HILAIRE WALDEN

Glorious PUDDINGS

HILAIRE WALDEN

Glorious PUDDINGS

CHARLES LETTS · Letts of London® · FOUNDED 1796

First published in 1992
by Charles Letts & Co Ltd
Letts of London House
Parkgate Road
London SW11 4NQ

Reprinted 1993

Designed and edited by
Anness Publishing Limited
Boundary Row Studios
1–7 Boundary Row
London SE1 8HP

Published in Australia by
J.B. Fairfax Press
Pty Limited
by arrangement with
Charles Letts & Co Ltd,
London, United Kingdom

ISBN 1 85238 353 4

A CIP catalogue record
for this book is available
from the British Library.

Editorial Director:
JOANNA LORENZ
Art Director:
PETER BRIDGEWATER
Project Editor:
JENNIFER JONES
Illustrations:
VANA HAGGERTY
Photographer:
KULBIR THANDI
Home Economist:
STEVEN WHEELER

Printed in Hong Kong
Reprinted 1993

Contents

INTRODUCTION

Serve a delicious looking, smelling and tasting honest-to-goodness pudding and watch people's faces light up. For there are few who do not agree with the sentiments of Maximillian Mission, a protestant exile who visited England at the end of the seventeenth century: 'Blessed be he that invented pudding for it is a manna that hits the palettes of all sorts of people'. Pudding as we know it – served at the end of the meal – was not, of course, invented but travelled, or evolved, from a simple, plain, starchy mixture served with, or as, the main course to fill empty stomachs cheaply. From about the beginning of the nineteenth century until about twenty years ago, a pudding was an integral part of every main meal. But changes in lifestyles and eating habits, poorer knowledge of cooking and, to some extent, concerns about calories and cholesterol have meant that, at best, puddings have become thought of as an indulgence, something for just once a week or for special occasions. For many, a proper, home-made pudding is a rarity and, I fear, many of the younger generation have never even had a moist, steaming Sticky Fig Pudding, or a slice of dark and deeply flavoured Parkin Pudding. On the other hand, I know some people who will happily forego the rest of a meal and just have a pudding, or two. A good pudding of some sort is the best way to end any meal on a high note. It does not have to be heavy or rich, require a long time slaving over a hot stove, and a large portion does not have to be eaten. 'Pudding' covers a wide range of dishes, but the one thing they all have in common is that they are not delicate, fanciful desserts, so none is overly expensive or complicated to make. In the following pages I have tried to supply recipes for many different occasions, to suit all tastes and budgets, and to take into account the time and degree of skill needed to prepare them.

A NOTE ON INGREDIENTS

BUTTER

The superiority of butter over margarine is distinguishable in puddings, and I think puddings justify its use, so I always use it. I have specified unsalted butter, because it is generally better quality and fresher than salted butter, and, again, I think this is reflected in the taste of a pudding.

CREAM

The richness of creams, in ascending order, is single, whipping, then double, and they can often be substituted for one another, as when making custard-type mixtures, depending on how rich you want a recipe to be. An exception is when cream has to be whipped, when only whipping or double cream can be used. Chill cream for whipping, use cold equipment and proceed cautiously, as cream can quite suddenly become curdled. For folding into mixtures, whip until the cream is thick enough just to form floppy peaks. If it is to be piped, it should be whisked until the whisk leaves stiff peaks when lifted from the cream.

EGGS

Eggs are used widely in all types of puddings, usually to add lightness, to thicken or set. They also add richness and flavour. It is important to use eggs that are good quality, which, for me, means free-range and fresh, especially in puddings where they are not cooked. Store eggs, pointed end down, in the refrigerator, but return them to room temperature about 30 minutes before they are used.

Where the size of the eggs is of importance, I have specified which to use. Where no size is mentioned, either size 1, 2 or 3 can be used.

SUGAR

Sugar has a more complex effect on a pudding than simply adding sweetness. It also influences the texture, and the choice of sugar can affect the flavour of the pudding. If the level of sugar is too high it will mask the other flavours. Bear in mind when cooking mixtures to be served cold that they will taste sweeter when hot than when cold.

NATURAL, UNREFINED BROWN SUGARS: golden granulated and golden caster as well as light muscovado, dark muscovado and demerara sugars, which are not refined to the same degree as white sugar, add a deeper flavour than plain white sugars and help to make puddings moist. Other brown sugars, called light, soft brown and dark soft brown, are fully refined white sugar to which colouring is added to darken them (some so-called demeraras are also treated in this way); packets of these will have a contents list on them, whereas packets of natural brown sugars will have their country of origin, such as Mauritius.

VANILLA SUGAR: vanilla sugar adds a subtle softness to the flavour of a pudding. It couldn't be easier to make – simply pop a vanilla pod in the sugar and keep it in an airtight container. Leave the sugar for about 5 days before using it. When the sugar has been used, add some more – the vanilla pod should remain effective for up to a year.

NUTS

Nuts add flavour to mixtures, and when chopped they add texture, and when they are ground they make mixtures moist. Nuts have a high oil content, so become stale and rancid quickly and lose flavour. These reactions occur more rapidly once the nuts have been removed from their shells and with even greater speed after they have been chopped or ground. So, where possible, buy nuts in their shells, or at least whole, keep them in the freezer, or a cool, dark, dry place for no longer than 1 month, and chop or grind them when you need them. Because of their high oil content, nuts become oily easily, so keep them cool when handling them, and when grinding them, do so in small amounts and take care not to overwork them. Normally, I use an old-fashioned hand rotary cheese grater, as I find it gives the best results, but if the nuts are to be mixed with flour or sugar, I sometimes mix these with the unground nuts and then grind small amounts in a blender or food processor.

Pour boiling water over the almonds to blanch

TO PEEL ALMONDS: put the nuts into a bowl, pour over boiling water, leave for a few minutes, then remove the nuts; the skin should slip off easily.

TO REMOVE THE THIN, BITTER INNER SKIN OF HAZELNUTS: place the nuts under a low grill or in a low oven until the skin dries and cracks, then tip the hot nuts into a clean cloth and rub until the papery skins come off.

Remove the nuts after a few minutes

TOASTING AND ROASTING NUTS: this enhances the flavour of nuts as well as adding a new dimension to it. Spread the nuts on a baking tray and place under a medium grill or in an oven set to 180°C/350°F/Gas 4 for 10–12 minutes, stirring occasionally, until the nuts have darkened evenly to the required degree.

CHOCOLATE

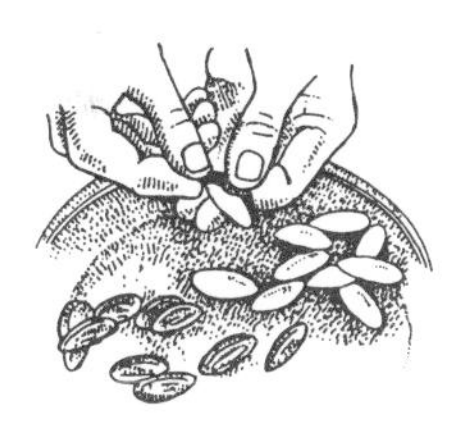

Split the nuts out of their skins

Chocolates vary not only in their quality but also in their sweetness. For the finest, most intense chocolatey flavour, use good quality confectioners' or bakers' chocolate, *chocolat pâtissier*, or the least sweet, darkest bitter type you can find. Bakers' chocolate may sometimes be referred to as cooking chocolate; chocolate-flavoured cake covering can also be euphemistically referred to as cooking chocolate as well, but it is quite a different product and to be avoided if you are hoping to make a good pudding.

Store chocolate in a cool, dry, dark place. For information about melting chocolate, see pages 134–135.

DRIED FRUITS

To most people the term dried fruit first means currants, raisins and sultanas, then perhaps apricots, prunes and figs. But many fruits are dried – peaches, pears and apple rings are quite easy to find, whilst searches in wholefood and Middle Eastern shops can reveal, for example, papayas, mangoes, sour and sweet cherries, and sheets of pineapple and raspberry fruit 'leathers'. All are well worth using in puddings, because they add interest and exciting new tastes.

The traditional way of drying fruits is to spread them out in the sun; the modern way is in tunnels of hot air, where, in fact, they may only be partially dried to become what is technically known as evaporated fruits. Their higher water content means they do not need to be soaked, but also that they will not keep as well as fully dried fruits. They are therefore usually treated with sulphur dioxide before drying, to help to give them a longer shelf-life and preserve their colour, then coated with vegetable oil or glucose syrup after drying to further help to preserve them and make them look attractively glossy. Appearances can be deceptive, though, as in the case of apricots, the best of which are Hunza apricots, which look pale and uninteresting compared with sulphurized no-need-to-soak ones. The best raisins are Muscatals, usually imported from Spain around Christmas. Because I prefer the dried fruits I eat to be dried traditionally, be untreated and to have a good flavour, I always buy them from a trustworthy wholefood shop with a good turnover. Unless they are to be cooked in a liquid, currants, sultanas and raisins can be soaked in a little wine, sherry, brandy, rum, whisky, apple juice or orange juice to plump them up before being used. When cooking other dried fruits, use only enough liquid to cover them. If there is a lot of surplus liquid at the end of the cooking, remove the fruit and boil the liquid until well reduced and syrupy, then pour back over the fruit.

Store all dried fruits in airtight containers in a cool, dry, dark place.

CANDIED, CRYSTALLIZED AND GLACE PEELS AND FRUITS

If you do not prepare your own candied, crystallized and glacé peel and fruits, it is well worth searching for good quality products; they can make a marked difference to your puddings when compared to results made using mass-produced brands found in supermarkets. Buy large slices of individual candied peels, as they have more flavour than chopped mixed peel, partly because there will have been less loss of the fragrant essential oils and partly because only the fattest, most juicy peels are sold whole. The delicate green variety of candied peel is made from the aromatic thick skin of the citron, a cousin of the lemon.

If pieces of candied peel are too sticky to be easily chopped, sprinkle them with a little of the flour from the recipe in which you are going to use them. If glacé fruits to be used in a steamed or baked sponge pudding are sticky, rinse them in warm water, then dry well, otherwise they will sink. As well as the more obvious high-class and speciality food shops, healthfood and wholefood shops often sell well-flavoured and succulent peels and fruits; and trips abroad can frequently lead to good finds.

Keep candied, crystallized and glacé fruits and peels in airtight containers in a cool, dry, dark place.

OVEN TEMPERATURES

Always set the oven thermostat to the correct temperature well in advance, remembering that the higher the temperature and the colder the atmosphere, the longer it will take for the oven to reach the required heat. Very few ovens have accurate thermostats – mine doesn't, I know, so I use an oven thermometer. But discrepancies between the temperature set on the dial and the one in the oven are only part of the story. The temperature might fluctuate by up to 37.5°C/100°F either side of the setting before the thermostat comes into operation, and, worse still, such fluctuations are not always constant. Outside factors, such as a general rise in the power consumption, can make an oven temperature drop suddenly and it may take a long time to return to the required level.

Most people become accustomed to the everyday peculiarities of their ovens and make adjustments to cooking temperatures and times given in recipes. This practice is all right for dishes such as casseroles, but with some sensitive patisseries it can result in failure and disappointment. So I would advise you to invest in an oven thermometer – it's worth it in the end. But even this does not do away with the need to keep an eye on the baking, because of the difficulty of being precise about timings.

A large pudding can cool the oven quite considerably, especially if the kitchen is not very warm and the ingredients and container in which the pudding is cooked are cold, so in these circumstances it is a good idea to preheat the oven to a slightly higher temperature than is needed, then turn the thermostat down to the correct setting when you put in the pudding.

QUANTITIES

The numbers I have given for how many people a pudding will serve are only guidelines, because not only do appetites for puddings in general differ, but they can be affected by how substantial the rest of the meal has been, the weather, time of day and occasion. And if you serve a pudding that is someone's, or more than one person's, favourite pudding the number can be reduced.

HOT BAKED PUDDINGS

CHAPTER ONE

Until the seventeenth century puddings were usually savoury, although they might contain dried fruits and spices and were sometimes served with sugar and almonds. As sugar became more widely available and fruit production improved, so sweet versions of puddings evolved and were specially created. In Britain, the royal seal of approval for puddings was given by 'the pudding-eating monarch', George I, who loved hearty, substantial sweet puddings. In fact, the British as a nation had a reputation for being pudding eaters, which was not usually meant as a term of flattery. (Even then, 'dessert' had other connotations. Derived from the French desservir, *meaning to clear the table, it was a selection of elaborate sweet dishes, fresh fruits, ices, fancy cakes and pastries and conserves.) But the culinary world would be much poorer without our beloved crumbles, charlottes, rice puddings, sponge puddings, bread and butter puddings – the list is long and richly varied.*

RIGHT (from top to bottom): Coconut and Mandarin Pudding (see page 61); Apple and Orange Surprise Crunch (see page 24); Maple Syrup and Grapefruit Pancakes (see page 76).

LEFT (from top to bottom): Light Apple Pudding (see page 51); Chocolate Truffle Loaf (see page 141); Greengage and Almond Shuttles (see page 103).

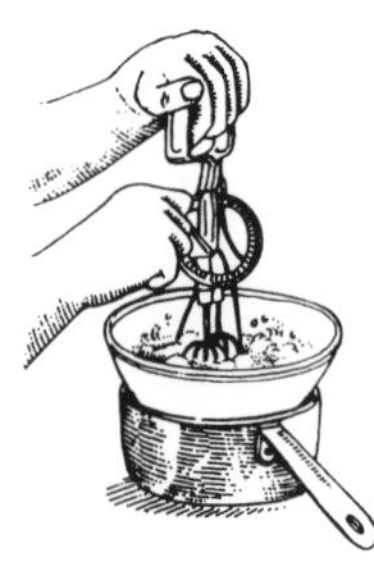

Whisk the egg yolks and sugar together in a bowl placed over a saucepan of hot water until the mixture is very thick and airy

Secrets of Success

☞ Unless a recipe specifies to the contrary, most puddings are best if they are baked as soon as they are prepared.
☞ To reduce the amount of work you have to do just before a meal, weigh out all the ingredients, do any preliminary preparation such as chopping nuts, lay out equipment and prepare baking containers in advance.
☞ Preheat the oven in plenty of time.
☞ Have ingredients and containers at room temperature, unless a recipe specifies to the contrary.
☞ To ensure puddings made by the creaming method are light, the butter and sugar must be beaten until they are light and fluffy, then eggs at room temperature gradually beaten in. Lastly, gently fold in the flour and any other ingredients using a large, cold metal spoon.
☞ If using a rotary whisk to whisk whole eggs or egg yolks with sugar to make a whisked sponge, place the bowl containing the eggs over a saucepan of hot, not boiling, water making sure the underside of the bowl is above the level of the water. If using an electric hand-held whisk, there is no need to place the bowl over a saucepan of hot water.
☞ Whisked egg whites help to lighten mixtures, but they must be folded into the mixture very carefully. Plain whisked whites are particularly fragile, so they are often whisked with some of the sugar from the recipe to make them firmer (see notes on making meringues on page 135).
☞ The heavier the main mixture, the more difficult it is to fold in egg whites, and for most puddings it is a good idea to fold in about a quarter of the whisked whites to lighten it, then fold in the rest in batches.
☞ Serve the pudding on hot or warm plates.

RHUBARB CHARLOTTE BETTY

SERVES 4–6

The difference between a fruit charlotte and a betty, both very popular traditional British puddings, is that a charlotte has a jacket of sliced bread and a betty has a lighter jacket of breadcrumbs. In a betty, breadcrumbs are also layered with the filling, which makes it more solid; spices may also be added. This recipe combines the breadcrumb jacket of a betty with the fruit-only filling of a charlotte. For extra flavour and crunch, I add sesame seeds.

- 3 Reinette or Cox's Orange Pippin apples
- 450 g/1 lb rhubarb, cut into approximately 2.5 cm/1 in lengths
- 55 ml/2 fl oz tangerine or orange juice
- 70 g/2½ oz light muscovado sugar
- 55 g/2 oz dark muscovado sugar
- ½ tsp Chinese five spice powder
- pinch of ground cloves
- pinch of freshly ground nutmeg
- 150 g/5 oz fresh breadcrumbs
- 3 tbsp sesame seeds, lightly toasted
- 85 g/3 oz unsalted butter, melted
- **To serve:**
- Custard (see page 181) or vanilla dairy ice cream

1 Set the oven to 180°C/350°F/Gas 4. Butter an 850 ml/1½ pint baking dish.

2 Peel, core and slice the apples, then mix with the rhubarb and tangerine or orange juice.

3 Stir the sugars and spices together. Mix 2 tablespoonfuls with the breadcrumbs, seasame seeds and butter, then press half evenly into the sides and base of the dish. Stir the remaining sugar mixture into the fruit, then spoon into the dish. Cover with the remaining breadcrumb mixture, cover loosely and bake for 20 minutes. Uncover and bake for 25 minutes until the fruit is tender and the top browned. Serve warm with Custard or vanilla dairy ice cream.

PEAR AND BLACKCURRANT CRUMBLE

SERVES 4 – 6

Crumbles are so easy to make that it is very difficult to make a bad one, and everyone I know loves them. It was very difficult to choose just one crumble recipe, because there are so many for toppings and fruit mixtures, as well as innumerable permutations – and I like them all, to the same degree! Friends were not much help; whatever I suggested was greeted by 'Oh yes, use that one'. So I wrote a list and stuck a pin in.

- 700 G/1 ½ LB PEARS
- 300 G/10 OZ BLACKCURRANTS, FRESH OR FROZEN, THAWED
- ABOUT 2 TBSP VANILLA SUGAR
- 115 G/4 OZ PLAIN FLOUR
- 85 G/3 OZ DEMERARA SUGAR
- 115 G/4 OZ UNSALTED BUTTER, DICED
- 115 G/4 OZ GROUND ALMONDS
- 2–3 TBSP SLIVERED ALMONDS
- **TO SERVE:**
- CUSTARD (SEE PAGE 181)

1 Set the oven to 180°C/350°F/Gas 4.

2 Peel, core and slice the pears and place in a 20–22.5 cm/8–9 inch shallow baking dish with the blackcurrants. Sprinkle over the vanilla sugar, according to the sweetness of the fruit and your taste.

3 Sift the flour into a mixing bowl, stir in the demerara sugar, add the butter and toss to coat in flour, then rub in until the mixture resembles breadcrumbs. Stir in the ground almonds.

4 Scatter evenly over the fruit, sprinkle over the slivered almonds, then press down lightly. Bake for about 40 minutes until the top is brown and the fruit cooked. Serve with Custard.

CARIBBEAN UPSIDE-DOWN PUDDING

SERVES 6

Lime, coconut and papaya are obvious flavours to bring together; add demerara sugar, and you have a pudding that evokes images of hot sunshine, balmy breezes, golden beaches, laughter and calypsos. If you can get knobbly Thai kaffir limes, use the rinds, but not the juice, as they have a really fragrant lime flavour.

- 2 PAPAYAS
- GRATED RIND AND JUICE OF 2 LIMES
- 85 G/3 OZ CASTER SUGAR
- 150 G/5 OZ DEMERARA SUGAR
- 115 G/4 OZ UNSALTED BUTTER
- 2 EGGS, SIZE 2, BEATEN
- 115 G/4 OZ PLAIN FLOUR
- 1½ TSP BAKING POWDER
- 25 G/1 OZ DESICCATED COCONUT
- **COCONUT SAUCE:**
- 300 ML/10 FL OZ DOUBLE CREAM
- 2 TBSP CASTER SUGAR, PREFERABLY VANILLA-FLAVOURED
- 55 G/2 OZ CREAMED COCONUT, CHOPPED
- 4 TBSP MILK
- **DECORATION:**
- LIGHTLY TOASTED FLAKED COCONUT

1 To make the sauce, pour the cream into a bowl. In a small saucepan, gently heat the sugar and coconut in the milk until the coconut and sugar have dissolved. Stir into the cream, then cover and place in the refrigerator to chill well.

2 Peel the papayas, cut in half and discard the seeds. Slice the papayas and place in a shallow dish. Sprinkle over the lime juice and leave for 2–3 hours.

3 Set the oven to 180°C/350°F/Gas 4. Well butter the base of a 24–25 cm/9½–10 inch fluted flan dish at least 4 cm/1½ inches deep, and butter the sides.

4 Drain the lime juice from the papaya slices into a bowl. Stir in the caster sugar and reserve for spooning over the baked pudding.

5 Arrange the papaya slices in the dish and sprinkle over 2 tablespoons of the demerara sugar.

6 Beat together the butter and the remaining demerara sugar until light and fluffy, then gradually beat in the eggs. Stir in the flour, baking powder, lime rind and coconut. Carefully spoon over the papaya slices and bake for about 50 minutes until a knife inserted in the centre comes out clean.

7 Prick the top of the pudding all over with a fine skewer or needle, stir the sweetened lime juice and spoon evenly over. Leave for a few minutes, then invert onto a warm plate. Sprinkle over flaked coconut to decorate and serve with the cold sauce.

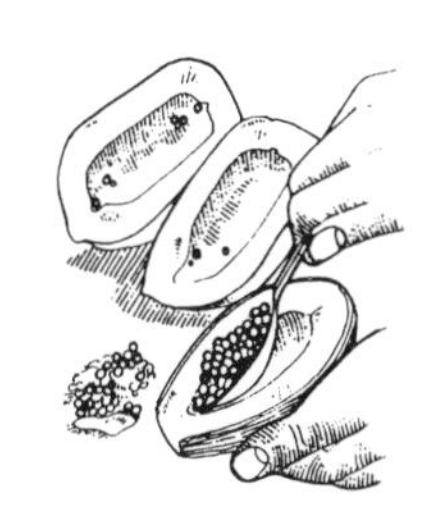

Use a spoon to scoop the seeds from the halved papaya

A PLUM PUDDING

SERVES 4

Not the *traditional British 'plum pudding', that is, Christmas Pudding , this simple, dare I say foolproof, recipe contains fresh plums beneath a light, moist and tender topping that is a cross between a custard and a sponge.*

- 550 G/1 1/4 LB RIPE PLUMS, HALVED AND STONED
- APPROXIMATELY 150 G/5 OZ VANILLA CASTER SUGAR
- 115 G/4 OZ GROUND ALMONDS
- 115 G/4 OZ UNSALTED BUTTER, MELTED AND COOLED
- 2 EGGS, SIZE 3, BEATEN
- 3 TBSP AMARETTO OR FEW DROPS ALMOND ESSENCE AND 2 TBSP SWEET SHERRY
- 150 ML/5 FL OZ MILK
- 25 G/1 OZ FLAKED ALMONDS
- ICING SUGAR, FOR DUSTING (OPTIONAL)

1 Set the oven to 180°C/350°F/Gas 4. Well butter the base of a 21.5 cm/8½ inch shallow baking dish, and butter the sides.

2 Place the plums in the dish and sprinkle with 1–2 tablespoons of the vanilla caster sugar, according to the sweetness of the plums and your taste.

3 Stir together the ground almonds, 115 g/4 oz sugar, the butter, eggs, amaretto or almond essence and sherry, and milk.

4 Spoon the almond mixture over the plums and sprinkle over the flaked almonds. Bake for 45–50 minutes until lightly set. Serve the pudding warm, dusted with icing sugar, if liked.

Illustrated opposite page 48

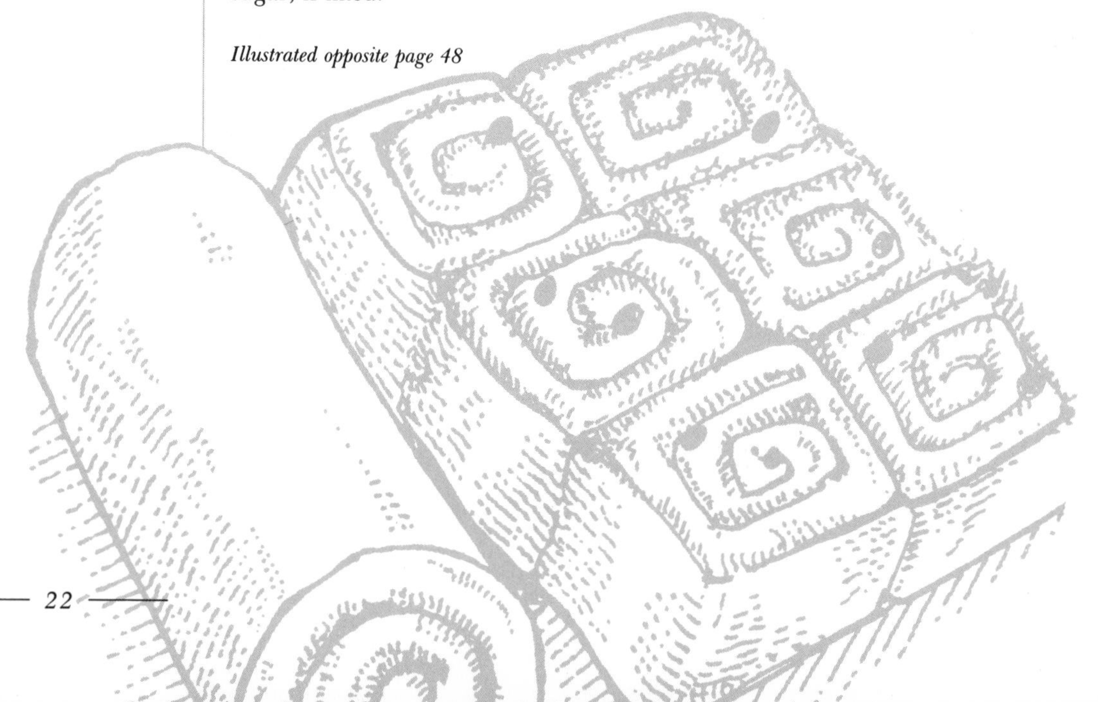

PRUNES BAKED IN A RICH CUSTARD

SERVES 4

This regal and easy-to-make pudding – a far cry from watery prunes swimming in a tasteless liquid served with a watery custard, which is a very distant, lowly cousin – has that special something that makes it irresistible, especially to me.

- 225 G/8 OZ LARGE, PLUMP PRUNES, SOAKED OVERNIGHT JUST COVERED BY WATER
- 5 TBSP ARMAGNAC, BRANDY OR WHISKY
- 225 G/8 OZ FULL-FAT SOFT CHEESE
- 85 ML/3 FL OZ DOUBLE OR WHIPPING CREAM
- 115 G/4 OZ VANILLA CASTER SUGAR
- FEW DROPS ALMOND ESSENCE
- FINELY GRATED RIND OF 1 LEMON
- 2 EGGS, SIZE 2, BEATEN
- 2 TBSP PLAIN FLOUR
- ICING SUGAR, FOR DUSTING

1 Cook the prunes in their soaking liquor until just tender. Drain the prunes from the liquid, cut them into halves and discard the stones. Place the prunes in a bowl, pour over the Armagnac, brandy or whisky, cover and leave for 2–3 hours.

2 Set the oven to 180°C/350°F/Gas 4. Butter a 675 ml/1¼ pint shallow, round baking dish.

3 Beat together the cheese, cream, sugar, almond essence and lemon rind until smooth, then mix in the eggs. Stir in the flour.

4 Drain the liquid from the prunes into the cheese mixture and stir in. Place the fruit in a single layer on the base of the dish and cover with the mixture. Bake for 30–35 minutes until lightly set in the centre.

5 Allow the pudding to cool for at least 30 minutes before serving lukewarm dusted with icing sugar.

VARIATION:

To make prunes in a rich, fluffy custard, divide the soaked prunes between 4 large individual ramekin dishes. Separate the eggs. Mix the yolks with the cheese, cream, sugar, almond essence and lemon rind. Whisk the egg whites and fold into the mixture (omit the flour). Divide between the dishes and bake for about 18 minutes.

Apple and Orange Surprise Crunch

SERVES 4

The surprise is the creamy layer between the crunchy oat topping and the piquant fruit base, all of which add up to a pudding that is interesting and tasty to eat. The creamy layer can be enriched by beating in about 55 g/2 oz full-fat soft cheese.

- 550 G/1 ¼ LB COOKING APPLES
- 1 ORANGE, PEELED, SLICED
- 1 TBSP FINELY CHOPPED FRESH GINGER
- 2–3 TBSP VANILLA CASTER SUGAR
- 2 TBSP WATER
- 2 EGGS, SIZE 2
- 300 ML/10 FL OZ CREAMY MILK
- 40 G/1 ½ OZ UNSALTED BUTTER, DICED
- 40 G/1 ½ OZ DARK MUSCOVADO SUGAR
- 70 G/2 ½ OZ ROLLED OATS

1 Set the oven to 180°C/350°F/Gas 4. Butter an approximately 22.5 cm/9 inch ovenproof dish.

2 Peel, core and slice the apples. Reserve a few slices and put the rest in the dish. Gently stir in the orange slices, finely chopped ginger and 1–2 tbsp of the vanilla caster sugar, to taste.

3 Place the reserved apple slices in a small saucepan with the water and poach gently until just tender. Remove with a slotted spoon and reserve.

4 Meanwhile, stir together the eggs and 1 tablespoon of the vanilla caster sugar in a medium-sized bowl. Bring the milk to the boil, stir into the egg mixture, then pour back into the saucepan and cook over a low heat, stirring constantly, until thickened; do not allow to boil. Pour over the fruit.

5 Gently heat the butter and muscovado sugar, stirring, until melted, then stir in the oats. Scatter over the custard and bake for about 35 minutes until the apple is tender and the topping brown and crisp.

6 Place the poached apple slices on top and serve hot.

Illustrated opposite page 16

Walnut and Date Pudding

SERVES 4

When you've had a bad day and everything seems to have gone wrong, or when simply feeling a little low, there's nothing like a pudding that's stood the test of time, like this one, to calm you down, buck you up and put things back into perspective.

- 175 G/6 OZ STONED DATES, COARSELY CHOPPED
- 115 ML/4 FL OZ BOILING WATER
- 2 EGGS, SEPARATED
- 55 G/2 OZ LIGHT MUSCOVADO SUGAR
- 85 G/3 OZ UNSALTED BUTTER, DICED
- 2 TBSP MAPLE SYRUP OR GOLDEN SYRUP
- 175 G/6 OZ PLAIN FLOUR
- 1 ½ TSP BAKING POWDER
- FEW DROPS VANILLA ESSENCE
- 85 G/3 OZ WALNUTS, ROUGHLY CHOPPED

1 Set the oven to 180°C/350°F/Gas 4. Butter a 1.2 litre/2 pint ovenproof dish. Put the dates in a bowl, pour over the boiling water, stir and leave to cool.

2 In a medium-sized bowl, whisk the egg yolks with the sugar until thick and fluffy. In a small saucepan, gently warm together the butter and syrup until the butter has melted. Allow it to cool slightly if very warm. Using a large metal spoon, gently fold the flour and baking powder into the egg yolk mixture with the syrup mixture, vanilla essence, walnuts and dates and their soaking liquid. In a clean, dry bowl, whisk the egg whites until stiff but not dry, then, using a large metal spoon, gently fold into the date mixture.

3 Pour into the dish and bake for about 1 hour until the pudding is springy to the touch in the centre.

IN THE STYLE OF QUEEN OF PUDDINGS

SERVES 4

I admit to being slightly devious when naming this recipe, as I wanted to attract both the many people who like Queen of Puddings and those who are less enamoured. Members of both camps who have tried this recipe have all become fans of it. The changes are subtle: I use an enriched bread, such as brioche; a little single cream in place of some of the milk; plenty of lemon, but not too much; and a very good, high-fruit content raspberry jam, often labelled as a 'conserve', which I boost with puréed raspberries for a fresher flavour or with eau-de-vie de framboise.

- 425 ML/15 FL OZ MILK
- 150 ML/5 FL OZ SINGLE CREAM
- 40 G/1½ OZ UNSALTED BUTTER
- 115 G/4 OZ BRIOCHE CRUMBS
- 3 EGGS, SEPARATED
- GRATED RIND OF 1 LARGE LEMON
- 55 G/2 OZ CASTER SUGAR, PLUS 1 TSP
- 2–4 TBSP GOOD QUALITY RASPBERRY JAM, WARMED
- 2–4 TBSP RASPBERRY PURÉE OR FEW DROPS *EAU-DE-VIE DE FRAMBOISE* OR FRAMBOISE LIQUEUR (OPTIONAL)

1 Bring the milk, cream and butter to simmering point, remove from the heat and stir in the brioche crumbs, egg yolks, lemon rind and half the sugar. Leave the mixture to stand for 30 minutes.

2 Set the oven to 170°C/325°F/Gas 3. Butter a 850 ml/1½ pint ovenproof dish.

3 Pour the crumb mixture into the dish and bake for about 45 minutes until lightly set in the centre.

4 If 'boosting' the raspberry jam, mix it with the raspberry purée or the eau-de-vie or liqueur.

5 Spread the jam over the pudding.

6 Whisk the egg whites until soft peaks form, then gradually whisk in the remaining sugar, whisking well after each addition, until the mixture is stiff and shiny. Pile onto the pudding, sprinkle over the teaspoon of sugar, and return to the oven for about 15 minutes until crisp and brown on top. Serve warm.

VARIATIONS:
If you want to go further and make a richer pudding, replace more of the milk with cream. Flavourings can be chopped candied peel, ground almonds or hazelnuts, desiccated coconut, rose water or orange flower water (omit the lemon rind), melted chocolate or cocoa powder (omit the lemon rind). Orange rind can be used instead of lemon rind, with orange segments in place of the jam. The breadcrumbs can be changed to plain cake crumbs, or the bread mixture can be poured over a fruit base.

MAGIC LIME PUDDING

SERVES 4

This is a new, more tangily fragrant version of the popular 'classic' lemon pudding that separates as if by magic during baking into a light, spongy layer floating on a sauce.

- 55 G/2 OZ UNSALTED BUTTER
- 115 G/4 OZ CASTER SUGAR
- FINELY GRATED RIND AND JUICE OF 3 LARGISH LIMES
- 2 EGGS, SEPARATED
- 55 G/2 OZ SELF-RAISING FLOUR
- 150 ML/5 FL OZ MILK

1 Set the oven to 180°C/350°F/Gas 4. Butter an 850 ml/1½ pint ovenproof dish.

2 Beat the butter, sugar and lime rind together until well softened (because there is more sugar than butter, the mixture will not become light and fluffy). Gradually beat in the egg yolks. Lightly fold in the flour alternately with the milk and lime juice. Whisk the egg whites until stiff but not dry, then, using a large metal spoon, gently fold into the butter mixture (don't worry if it looks a little curdled at this stage – it's quite normal). Pour into the dish and bake for 40–45 minutes until golden and the sponge is just set.

Illustrated opposite page 64

Rice 'Gâteau'

SERVES 4

Rice pudding has many different faces, ranging from the school meals version, which should be served hot but is invariably tepid, to extravagant, refined, moulded creations of French 'haute cuisine', which are served cold. The presentation of this version is quite unlike any other – served hot, it is 'moulded' so that it can be turned out like a cake and has a consistency somewhere between that of a soufflé and a light sponge, with a fairly soft, creamy centre and a crisp outside. It has a certain elegance, yet it is still 'homely', hence the name – to call it 'Rice Cake' would not convey the right impression. Coconut milk (see page 88) and almond milk (see page 167) produce very interesting variations. If time allows, soak the rice in the milk for a couple of hours.

- 550 ML/1 PINT CREAMY MILK OR MILK AND SINGLE CREAM, MIXED
- 100 G/3½ OZ PUDDING RICE
- 70 G/2½ OZ VANILLA SUGAR
- 40 G/1½ OZ UNSALTED BUTTER
- FINELY GRATED RIND OF 1 LEMON
- 40 G/1½ OZ BRIOCHE, CHOLLA OR OTHER GOOD BREADCRUMBS
- SPRINKLING ICING SUGAR
- 3 EGGS, SEPARATED
- FEW DROPS ROSE WATER
- **TO SERVE:**
- CHERRY COMPOTE (SEE PAGE 49), PLUM AND RASPBERRY COMPOTE (SEE PAGE 87), APRICOT SAUCE (SEE PAGE 187) OR LIGHTLY SWEETENED, SIEVED RASPBERRIES

1 Put the milk and rice into a heavy-based saucepan and bring to just below simmering point. Stir in the sugar and butter and simmer gently, stirring occasionally, for about 30 minutes until the rice is swollen and creamy. Stir in the lemon rind and leave to cool slightly.

2 Set the oven to 140°C/275°F/Gas 1. Well butter an 850 ml/1½ pint soufflé dish. Mix the breadcrumbs with a little icing sugar, then press evenly into the sides and base so there are no gaps.

3 Beat the egg yolks and rose water into the rice.

4 In a clean, dry bowl, whisk the egg whites until stiff but not dry, then, using a large metal spoon, gently fold into the rice mixture in three batches. Gently pour into the dish, taking care not to dislodge the crumb coating. Bake for 1 hour 20 minutes until just firm to the touch in the centre and the top is crisp and golden. Serve from the dish or turn out onto a warm plate and serve with Cherry Compote, Plum and Raspberry Compote, Apricot Sauce or lightly sweetened, sieved raspberries.

Christmas Pudding Soufflé

SERVES 4

I like Christmas pudding and will eat it all year round (I find it difficult to resist puddings sold post-Christmas at reduced prices), providing the pudding is a good one. During the course of my researches to find good puddings, despite exercising my experience of the subject, which enables me to reject the really bad ones, I end up with some that I feel would benefit from a little 'doctoring' – and this is what I do with them.

- 225 G/8 OZ CHRISTMAS PUDDING, CRUMBLED
- 3 TBSP RUM, WHISKY OR BRANDY
- 2 TBSP DOUBLE OR WHIPPING CREAM OR MILK
- 4 EGGS, SIZE 2, SEPARATED
- 1 EXTRA EGG WHITE, SIZE 2
- 25–55 G/1–2 OZ VANILLA CASTER SUGAR, DEPENDING ON THE SWEETNESS OF THE PUDDING

- **TO SERVE:**
- CREAM, VANILLA DAIRY ICE CREAM, ICED MASCARPONE (SEE PAGE 80) OR SABAYON SAUCE (SEE PAGE 185)

1 If you have an hour or so before you need to start to make the pudding, put the Christmas pudding into a shallow dish, sprinkle over the rum, whisky or brandy and leave to soak.

2 Set the oven to 200°C/400°F/Gas 6. Butter 4 individual soufflé or ramekin dishes.

3 Put the Christmas pudding into a mixing bowl, add the cream or milk, egg yolks, and rum, whisky or brandy if the pudding has not been soaked in it, and beat together to remove large lumps but so the mixture is a little nobbly.

4 In a clean, dry bowl, whisk the egg whites until soft peaks form, then gradually whisk in the sugar, whisking well after each addition, until the mixture is stiff and shiny. Using a large metal spoon, gently fold about a quarter into the Christmas pudding mixture to loosen it, then lightly fold in the remainder.

5 Fill the dishes to their rim, then run a spoon, knife or fork handle between the pudding and the dish so the mixture will rise upwards rather than flow over the sides. Bake for about 25–30 minutes until well risen, and lightly set. To serve, make a small hole in the top and pour or spoon in cream, vanilla dairy ice cream, Iced Mascarpone or Sabayon Sauce.

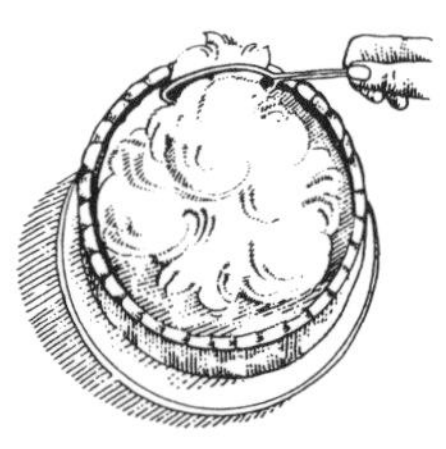

Spoon the meringue over the custard and swirl into peaks

PEACH MERINGUE PUDDING

SERVES 6

My grandmother's speciality was a pineapple pudding and, as she grew older and cooked less, she would make it, or suggest making it, for any occasion that was not part of normal daily life. A simple dessert, it consisted of canned pineapple, a cornflour custard enriched with egg yolks and flavoured with vanilla essence, and a meringue topping. Peach Meringue Pudding belongs to the same family, but the fruit is fresh, the custard is thickened only with egg yolks and a vanilla pod replaces the essence. I know Grandmother would have approved.

- 425 ML/15 FL OZ MILK, OR A MIXTURE OF MILK AND CREAM
- 1 VANILLA POD
- 3 EGGS, SEPARATED
- 2 EGG YOLKS
- 125 G/4½ OZ VANILLA CASTER SUGAR
- 20 G/¾ OZ UNSALTED BUTTER
- 1½ TBSP LIGHT MUSCOVADO SUGAR
- 4 PEACHES
- APPROXIMATELY 2 TBSP LEMON JUICE
- 1 TBSP KIRSCH (OPTIONAL)
- 2–3 TBSP FLAKED ALMONDS

1 In a heavy-based saucepan, gently heat the milk with the vanilla pod to just on simmering point. Remove from the heat, cover and leave for 20 minutes.

2 In a medium-sized bowl, beat the egg yolks with about 1 tablespoon of the vanilla caster sugar. Bring the milk to the boil, then stir into the egg yolk mixture. Return to the saucepan and heat very gently, stirring with a wooden spoon, until thickened; do not allow to boil. Remove the vanilla pod.

3 Set the oven to 190°C/375°F/Gas 5. Spread the butter over the base of a wide 1.2–1.5 litre/2–2½ pint ovenproof dish and sprinkle with the light muscovado sugar.

4 If the peaches are very ripe, the skin should easily peel off. If it clings stubbornly to the fruit, place the peaches in a bowl, cover with boiling water, leave for about 20 seconds, then drain off the water – the skin should then come away without any problem. Thickly slice the peaches and discard the stones. Place the peach slices in a frying pan, cover with cold water and bring to simmering point. Poach gently for 5–10 minutes until tender. Drain and place in the dish. Sprinkle over the lemon juice and the kirsch, if using.

5 In a clean, dry bowl, whisk the egg whites until soft peaks form, then gradually whisk in the remaining sugar, whisking well after each addition, until the mixture is stiff and shiny. Spoon over the custard. Scatter over the flaked almonds and bake for 12–15 minutes until brown and crisp on top. Serve warm.

APPLE AND BLACKBERRY FLAPJACK

SERVES 6

The chewy, oaty flapjack jacket packed with seasonal apples and blackberries provides compensation for the colder days and longer nights of autumn.

- 550 G/1 ¼ LB COOKING APPLES
- 25 G/1 OZ CASTER OR GRANULATED SUGAR
- 550 G/1 ¼ LB BLACKBERRIES
- 40 G/1 ½ OZ DARK MUSCOVADO SUGAR
- 150 G/5 OZ UNSALTED BUTTER, DICED
- 4 TBSP GOLDEN SYRUP
- 200 G/7 OZ ROLLED OATS
- 40 G/1 ½ OZ SUNFLOWER SEEDS
- 1 ¼ TSP GROUND CINNAMON
- **DECORATION:**
- POACHED APPLE RINGS, OR BLACKBERRIES AND ICING SUGAR
- **TO SERVE:**
- CUSTARD (SEE PAGE 181)

1 Set the oven to 190°C/375°F/Gas 5. Butter a 20 cm/8 inch springform cake tin, line with greaseproof paper, then butter the paper.

2 Peel, core and slice the apples, then very gently simmer with the caster or granulated sugar in a covered saucepan until soft. Stir in the blackberries and leave to cool slightly.

3 Gently heat the dark muscovado sugar, butter and golden syrup, stirring occasionally, until the sugar has dissolved and the butter melted. Stir in the oats, sunflower seeds and cinnamon. Use three-quarters to line the cake tin, taking the mixture to about 2.5 cm/1 inch from the rim. Pour in the apple and blackberries, then cover with the remaining oat mixture, pressing it down lightly. Bake for about 35 minutes.

4 Allow to cool for 10 minutes before loosening the edges and removing the pudding from the tin. Decorate with poached apple rings, or blackberries and icing sugar. Serve warm with Custard.

Omelette Norvégienne

SERVES 4–6

Omelette Norvégienne is less well known than baked Alaska, but it is very similar and, I think, much better. The addition of whisked yolks to the egg whites gives them body without requiring the same amount of sugar as the meringue for a baked Alaska, and makes a more rounded and successful dish. The ice cream must be really hard before starting. Other fruits can, of course, be used in place of the blackcurrants.

- 225 G/8 OZ BLACKCURRANTS, FRESH OR FROZEN, THAWED
- 2 TBSP WATER
- 2 TBSP CASTER SUGAR
- 2 TBSP WHITE RUM
- 3 EGGS, SEPARATED
- 1 × 17.5 CM/7 INCH OBLONG SPONGE CAKE
- 550 ML/1 PINT HOME-MADE OR VANILLA DAIRY ICE CREAM
- CASTER SUGAR, FOR SPRINKLING

1 Set the oven to 220°C/425°F/Gas 7.

2 Gently heat the blackcurrants with the water and half the sugar in a fairly small, covered saucepan, shaking the pan occasionally, until the fruit juices just begin to run. Add the white rum, then leave uncovered until cold.

3 Whisk the egg yolks and remaining sugar together until thick and creamy. In a clean, dry bowl, and using a clean whisk, whisk the egg whites until stiff but not dry. Using a large metal spoon, gently fold the egg whites into the yolks.

4 Place the sponge on a large ovenproof serving plate. Spoon over the blackcurrants and juices then place the ice cream on top, trimming to fit, if necessary. Quickly cover the ice cream and cake completely with the egg mixture. Sprinkle with caster sugar and bake for 3 minutes until the top is golden. Serve at once.

RIGHT (from top to bottom): Jaqui's Bread and Butter Pudding (see page 50); Omelette Norvégienne; Apricot Pandowdy (see page 45).

GLAZED NECTARINE SLICES

SERVES 2–4

The butter and sugar melt and bathe the nectarines and brioche in a spicy, butterscotch glaze. In place of the whole seeds, you could use about half a teaspoon of Chinese five spice powder, which is sold by a major British food company and is available in supermarkets.

- 2 RIPE BUT FIRM NECTARINES
- 2–4 SLICES OF BRIOCHE, OR OTHER GOOD, FIRM BREAD SUCH AS CHOLLA OR VIENNA, DEPENDING ON SIZE, CRUSTS REMOVED
- APPROXIMATELY 55 G/2 OZ UNSALTED BUTTER
- ½ TSP CORIANDER SEEDS
- ½ TSP SZECHUAN PEPPERCORNS
- ⅓ CINNAMON STICK
- APPROXIMATELY 55 G/2 OZ LIGHT MUSCOVADO SUGAR
- APPROXIMATELY 3 TBSP FLAKED ALMONDS (OPTIONAL)
- **TO SERVE:**
- ORANGE BUTTER SAUCE (SEE PAGE 186), ICED MASCARPONE (SEE PAGE 80), SABAYON SAUCE (SEE PAGE 185), CREAM, VANILLA DAIRY ICE CREAM OR STRAINED GREEK YOGURT

1 Set the oven to 180°C/350°F/Gas 4. Butter a shallow baking sheet.

2 Place the nectarines in a bowl, pour over boiling water and leave for about 30 seconds. Remove the nectarines from the water, then peel off the skins and cut each nectarine in half and remove the stone.

3 Cut the slices of bread in half if they are large. Generously butter one side of each slice of bread.

4 Crush the spices together very finely. Mix with the sugar and sprinkle some over the buttered side of the bread.

5 Place a nectarine half, cut-side down, on the buttered and sugared side of each piece of bread and cut deep slashes in the fruit. Insert slivers of butter in the slashes, scatter over the almonds, if using, and sprinkle generously with the remainder of the sugar and spice mixture. Lay the slices on the baking sheet and bake for about 15 minutes until the bread is crisp and browned at the edges, the fruit softened and coated in sauce. Serve warm with Orange Butter Sauce, Iced Mascarpone, Sabayon Sauce, cream, vanilla dairy ice cream or strained Greek yogurt.

LEFT (from top to bottom): Charlie's Apple Dappy (see page 53); Hot Orange Cake (see page 34); Glazed Nectarine Slices.

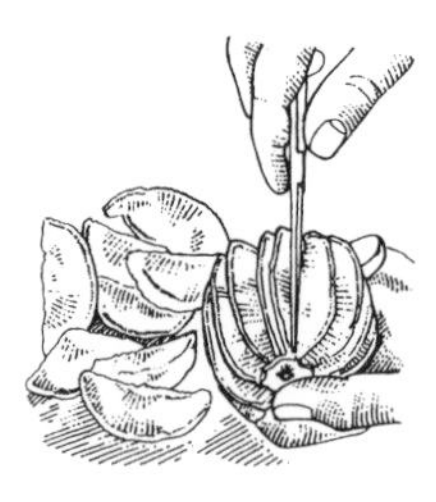

Holding the orange over a bowl, cut down between the flesh and the membrane to remove the segments

HOT ORANGE CAKE

SERVES 6

The tangy soured cream filling melts deliciously into the hot cake, so it should be served quickly. The syrup is really meant to be optional as the pudding is sufficiently good without it, but I always seem to be able to find the few seconds needed to make it – and on occasions (not just special ones!) I add some Cointreau. Around Christmas, tangerines or satsumas can be substituted for the oranges.

- 115 G/4 OZ UNSALTED BUTTER
- 115 G/4 OZ CASTER SUGAR
- 2 LARGE EGGS, SEPARATED
- 115 G/4 OZ SELF-RAISING FLOUR
- JUICE AND FINELY GRATED RIND OF 3 SMALL ORANGES
- 225 ML/8 FL OZ SOURED CREAM
- FRESH ORANGE SEGMENTS WITH ALL THE PITH AND SKIN REMOVED
- ICING SUGAR, FOR SIFTING (OPTIONAL)
- **SYRUP (OPTIONAL):**
- 5 TBSP ORANGE JUICE
- 1 TBSP COINTREAU (OPTIONAL)
- 7–8 TBSP ICING SUGAR

1 Set the oven to 180°C/350°F/Gas 4. Butter a 20 cm/8 inch springform or non-stick cake tin.

2 Beat together the butter and 85 g/3 oz of sugar until light and fluffy. Beat in the egg yolks, then stir in half the flour and the juice and rind of 1 orange.

3 In a clean, dry bowl, whisk the egg whites until soft peaks form, then gradually whisk in the remaining sugar. Using a large metal spoon, gently fold into the orange mixture with the remaining flour. Spoon into the tin and bake for 20–30 minutes until golden and springy to the touch.

4 Meanwhile, lightly beat the soured cream with the remaining orange juice and finely grated rind.

5 To make the syrup, if using, gently warm the orange juice, Cointreau, if using, and icing sugar in a small saucepan just before the cake is cooked.

6 Remove the cake from the oven, leave for 2 minutes, then turn out and cut in half horizontally using a bread knife. Quickly prick the top of the cake all over, then brush with the syrup, if used, and spread the soured cream over the bottom half, then cover with the top half. Top with orange segments, sift icing sugar over if the syrup has not been used and serve while the cake is still very warm.

Illustrated opposite page 33

FRANGIPANE CUSTARD

SERVES 4 – 6

Luxurious to eat, yet simplicity itself to make, this is an all-round popular pudding.

- 85 G/3 OZ BLANCHED ALMONDS, GROUND
- 85 G/3 OZ UNSALTED BUTTER, MELTED AND COOLED
- 425 ML/15 FL OZ SINGLE CREAM
- 85 G/3 OZ VANILLA CASTER SUGAR
- 4 EGGS, SIZE 2, BEATEN
- FINELY GRATED RIND AND JUICE OF ½ LEMON
- FEW DROPS VANILLA ESSENCE
- 3 TBSP AMARETTO
- **TO SERVE:**
- FRESH RASPBERRIES, SLICED STRAWBERRIES SPRINKLED WITH SUGAR, COLD CHERRY COMPOTE (SEE PAGE 49) OR COLD PLUM AND RASPBERRY COMPOTE (SEE PAGE 87)

1 Set the oven to 180°C/350°F/Gas 4. Butter an approximately 22.5 cm/9 inch shallow baking dish.

2 Stir together all the ingredients. Pour into the dish and bake for about 30–35 minutes until *very* lightly set in the centre. Serve warm with fresh raspberries, sliced strawberries sprinkled with just a little sugar to draw out their juices, cold Cherry Compote or cold Plum Compote.

Lining the base of a tin:

Place the tin on greaseproof paper and draw its outline on the paper

Butter the tin

Fit the paper into the tin

SUCCULENT, SMOOTH APPLE CAKE

SERVES 6–8

Unlike most apple cakes, which contain pieces of apple either folded into or placed on the top or bottom of a creamed or rubbed in cake mixture, this moist and tasty cake contains a fresh-tasting apple purée, which is simply stirred in to nearly all the remaining ingredients, leaving just the whisking of egg whites to be done.

- 450 G/1 LB BRAMLEY APPLES
- 1 TBSP WATER
- STRIP ORANGE OR LEMON PEEL
- 175 G/6 OZ LIGHT MUSCOVADO SUGAR
- 2 EGGS, SEPARATED
- 150 ML/5 FL OZ SUNFLOWER OR LIGHT OLIVE OIL
- 225 G/8 OZ SELF-RAISING FLOUR
- 1½ TSP GROUND CINNAMON
- 1½ TSP GROUND GINGER
- 85 G/3 OZ PLUMP RAISINS
- **TO SERVE:**
- ORANGE BUTTER SAUCE (SEE PAGE 186), FLUFFY ORANGE SAUCE (SEE PAGE 184), SABAYON SAUCE (SEE PAGE 185), CUSTARD (SEE PAGE 181) OR ORANGE CUSTARD (SEE PAGE 182)

1 Peel, core and chop the apples, then cook gently in a covered saucepan with the water, citrus peel and 25 g/1 oz of the sugar, shaking the pan occasionally, until the apples are soft.

2 Set the oven to 180°C/350°F/Gas 4. Butter and flour a 20 cm/8 inch cake tin and line the base with non-stick silicone paper.

3 Discard the citrus peel from the apple, then purée the apples with 70 g/2½ oz of the sugar, the egg yolks and oil. Sift together the flour and spices, then lightly mix into the apple mixture with the raisins.

4 In a clean, dry bowl, whisk the egg whites until soft peaks form, then gradually whisk in the remaining sugar, whisking well after each addition, until the mixture is stiff and shiny. Using a large metal spoon, gently fold into the apple mixture. Transfer to the tin and bake for 35–40 minutes until golden and springy to the touch in the centre. Serve with Orange Butter Sauce, Fluffy Orange Sauce, Sabayon Sauce, Custard or Orange Custard.

Illustrated opposite page 161

BLACKBERRY MERINGUE SHORTBREAD CAKE

SERVES 8

The blackberries, sitting on a melt-in-the-mouth shortbread base and covered by a billowy meringue that is crisp outside but soft inside, are deliciously warm and just yielding their juice, so neither their texture nor their taste are spoilt by cooking. A subtle flavouring of rose water will enhance the flavour of the blackberries, adding a special flavour and fragrance that is both slightly exotic and very traditionally English.

- 450 G/1 LB BLACKBERRIES
- 40 G/1 ½ OZ CASTER SUGAR
- **SHORTBREAD CAKE:**
- 175 G/6 OZ UNSALTED BUTTER, SOFTENED
- 115 G/4 OZ CASTER SUGAR
- 4 EGG YOLKS, SIZE 2
- 85 G/3 OZ ALMONDS, GROUND
- 250 G/9 OZ SELF-RAISING FLOUR
- **MERINGUE:**
- 4 EGG WHITES, SIZE 2
- 115 G/4 OZ CASTER SUGAR
- ROSE WATER, TO TASTE

1 Set the oven to 190°C/375°F/Gas 5. Butter a 25 cm/10 inch loose-based flan tin.

2 To make the cake, beat the butter with the sugar until pale and creamy, then gradually beat in the egg yolks. Using a large metal spoon, gently fold in the ground almonds and the flour. Spread evenly in the tin, then bake for about 30 minutes until a light fawn colour and just firm to the touch in the centre.

3 Gently mix together the blackberries and sugar, then place in an even layer on the cake, leaving a 1.25 cm/½ inch border all the way round.

4 To make the meringue, in a large, clean, dry bowl, whisk the egg whites until soft peaks form, then gradually whisk in the sugar, whisking well after each addition, until the mixture is stiff and shiny. Whisk in rose water to taste with the last of the sugar. Spoon over the blackberries and the border around the edge of the cake to seal in the fruit. Use the back of a spoon to swirl the top of the meringue into soft peaks. Turn the oven temperature up to 220°C/425°F/Gas 7 and bake for 5–10 minutes until the meringue is just firm and the peaks lightly browned.

Illustrated opposite page 64

MOCHA PUDDING WITH FUDGE-MUD SAUCE

SERVES 4–6

A wonderfully rich, chocolatey, fudgy variation on the theme of a spongy pudding sitting on a self-made sauce.

- 115 G/4 OZ LIGHT MUSCOVADO SUGAR
- 115 G/4 OZ SELF-RAISING FLOUR
- ½ TSP BAKING POWDER
- 1 TBSP COCOA POWDER
- 55 G/2 OZ UNSALTED BUTTER, DICED
- APPROXIMATELY 1½ TBSP INSTANT COFFEE GRANULES
- 150 ML/5 FL OZ MILK
- 1 TSP VANILLA ESSENCE
- **SAUCE:**
- 225 G/8 OZ DEMERARA SUGAR
- 5 TBSP COCOA POWDER
- 425 ML/15 FL OZ MILK

1 Set the oven to 180°C/350°F/Gas 4. Butter a deep 1.5 litre/2½ pint ovenproof dish.

2 Stir together the sugar, flour, baking powder and cocoa powder. Gently heat the butter and coffee granules in the milk until the butter has melted, then gradually beat into the dry ingredients and add the vanilla essence. Pour into the dish.

3 To make the sauce, mix together the sugar and cocoa powder, then scatter evenly over the top of the pudding mixture. Pour over the milk. Bake for about 1 hour until the sponge is set throughout.

HAZELNUT AND BERRY SHORTCAKE

SERVES 6

This pudding, which has a soft hazelnutty centre surrounding moist fruit, is equally good made using either raspberries, loganberries or blackberries. The apple can be added raw, as in the recipe, so that it still has some texture at the end of the baking, or it can first be gently cooked in a covered saucepan, shaking the pan occasionally, until softened, then left to cool. For flavourings, I like to include orange flower water either with the fruit or the hazelnut mixture, or I mix ground cinnamon with the caster sugar sprinkled over the baked shortcake.

- 150 G/5 OZ UNSALTED BUTTER, DICED
- 150 G/5 OZ VANILLA SUGAR
- 1 EGG, BEATEN
- 150 G/5 OZ HAZELNUTS, GROUND
- 150 G/5 OZ SELF-RAISING FLOUR
- 175 G/6 OZ EATING APPLES, SUCH AS COX'S ORANGE PIPPINS OR REINETTES
- 300 G/10 OZ FRESH BERRIES
- CASTER SUGAR, FOR SPRINKLING
- **TO SERVE:**
- DOUBLE CREAM OR STRAINED GREEK YOGURT

1 Set the oven to 180°C/350°F/Gas 4. Butter a 22.5 cm/8½ inch loose-based deep flan tin.

2 Beat together the butter, sugar and egg until well mixed. Stir in the hazelnuts and flour. Spread half in the base of the flan tin, using a fork to flatten lightly.

3 Peel, core and finely chop the apples. Mix with the berries, then place in an even layer on the hazelnut mixture. Dot over the remaining hazelnut mixture so that the fruit is almost covered.

4 Place on a baking sheet and bake for about 1 hour, covering lightly when well browned. The cake should feel *just* firm, with a springy texture. Remove from the oven, but leave in the tin for about 1 hour. Sprinkle over caster sugar and serve warm with double cream or strained Greek yogurt.

MOTHER'S MINCEMEAT PUDDING

SERVES 4

Like many other people, my mother always buys and makes far too much food at Christmas. Mince pies, and the ingredients for making yet more mince pies, is a particular foible. Consequently, there is always a supply of mincemeat left in the larder, which is transformed very effectively into this delicious, tasty pudding. If you have good, moist, home-made mincemeat, the apple and brandy should not be needed.

- 1 Bramley apple (optional)
- 225 g/8 oz mincemeat
- finely grated rind of 1 orange
- 2–3 tbsp brandy (optional)
- 85 g/3 oz unsalted butter
- 70 g/2½ oz dark muscovado sugar
- 2 eggs, beaten
- 115 g/4 oz self-raising flour
- **To serve:**
- Custard (see page 181) or vanilla dairy ice cream

1 Set the oven to 160°C/325°F/Gas 3. Butter an approximately 20 cm/8 inch round, shallow baking dish.

2 Peel, core and grate the apple, if using. Mix with the mincemeat, orange rind and brandy, if using.

3 Beat together the butter and sugar until light and fluffy, then gradually beat in the eggs, beating well after each addition. Using a large metal spoon, lightly fold in the flour, then the mincemeat mixture. Spoon into the dish and bake for 10 minutes.

4 Lower the oven temperature to 150°C/300°F/Gas 2 and bake for a further 40–45 minutes until set in the centre. Serve hot with Custard or vanilla dairy ice cream.

Illustrated opposite page 48

BAKED APPLES WITH A MIDDLE EASTERN FLAVOUR

SERVES 6

The special yet simple combination of ingredients in the filling, together with the honey-sweetened, fragrant, buttery citrus basting juices, give an exotic, luxurious air to an everyday pudding that is hard to resist.

- 6 LARGE EATING APPLES
- 40 G/1 ½ OZ DRIED FIGS, FINELY CHOPPED
- 40 G/1 ½ OZ STONED, NO-NEED-TO-SOAK PRUNES, FINELY CHOPPED
- 40 G/1 ½ OZ WALNUTS, CHOPPED
- 2 TBSP FINELY CHOPPED STEM GINGER
- 1 TSP FINELY GRATED LEMON RIND
- 1 TBSP APRICOT PRESERVE
- ¼ TSP FRESHLY GROUND CINNAMON
- 25 G/1 OZ UNSALTED BUTTER
- 115 G/4 OZ CLEAR HONEY
- 85 ML/3 FL OZ ORANGE JUICE
- 1 TBSP LEMON JUICE
- FINELY CRUSHED SEEDS FROM 3 CARDAMOM PODS

1 Set the oven to 180°C/350°F/Gas 4.

2 Core the apples and slightly enlarge the cavities. Score a fine line around the circumference of each apple. Place in a shallow baking dish they just fit.

3 In a bowl, beat together the figs, prunes, walnuts, ginger, lemon rind, apricot preserve and cinnamon until well combined. Pack the mixture into the cavities in the apples.

4 In a small saucepan, gently heat the butter, honey, orange juice, lemon juice and cardamom seeds, stirring with a wooden spoon, until the butter has melted and the mixture is smooth. Pour over the apples and bake for about 45 minutes, basting every 10 minutes or so with the cooking juices, until the apples are soft. Serve with the cooking juices spooned over.

Illustrated opposite page 49

Butter a kugelhopf mould or fancy ring cake mould

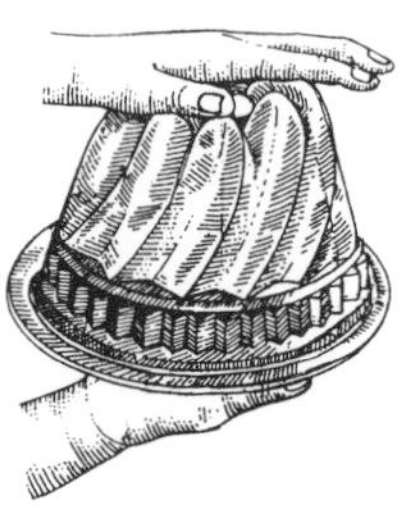

To turn out the pudding, place a warm plate over the top of the mould, hold the mould and plate firmly together, then invert them

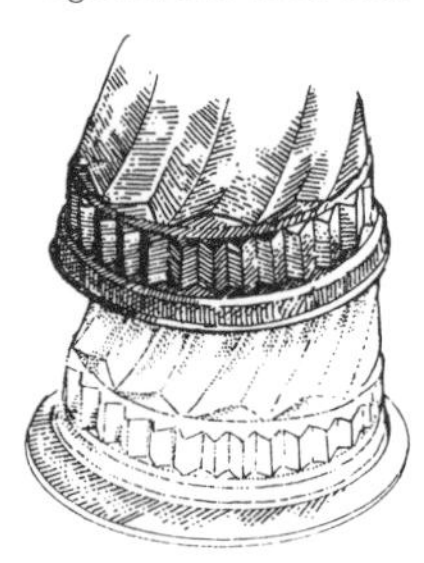

Carefully lift away the mould

HAZELNUT PRALINE SOUFFLÉ PUDDING

SERVES 4 – 6

This is an extremely moreish but quite light and not-too-sweet pudding. I first made it using hazelnut biscuits, but I thought the addition of small pieces of chocolate speckled through it might be an improvement. The nearest biscuits I could find contained chocolate chips, and they worked very well. You could, of course, buy hazelnut biscuits and chop some chocolate yourself.

- 100 G/3½ OZ UNSALTED BUTTER, SOFTENED
- 4 EGGS, SEPARATED
- 125 ML/4½ FL OZ MILK
- 25 G/1 OZ HAZELNUTS, ROASTED, SKINNED AND GROUND
- 125 G/4½ OZ HAZELNUT AND CHOCOLATE CHIP BISCUITS, CRUSHED
- 25 G/1 OZ SELF-RAISING FLOUR
- **PRALINE:**
- 125 G/4½ OZ CASTER SUGAR
- 100 G/3½ OZ HAZELNUTS, SKINNED
- **TO SERVE:**
- CUSTARD (SEE PAGE 181) OR VANILLA DAIRY ICE CREAM

1 To make the praline, in a small heavy-based saucepan, gently heat 100 g/3½ oz of the sugar and the skinned nuts without stirring, until the sugar melts. Increase the heat and cook until the mixture turns a rich brown colour, tossing the pan occasionally to prevent the nuts sticking. Tip quickly into a thin layer on a baking tray and leave until cold. Crush using a rolling pin and either continue crushing with the rolling pin to make a coarse powder, or use a food processor.

2 Set the oven to 190°C/375°F/Gas 5. Butter a 1.5 litre/2½ pint kugelhopf mould or fancy cake ring mould and place in a baking tin.

3 Beat the butter with the praline until pale and creamy, then whisk in the egg yolks, followed by the milk. Using a large metal spoon, lightly fold in the ground hazelnuts, biscuits and flour.

4 In a clean, dry bowl, whisk the egg whites until soft peaks form, then gradually whisk in the remaining sugar, whisking well after each addition, until the mixture is stiff and shiny. Using a large metal spoon, gently fold into the hazelnut mixture, then spoon into the mould and cover the top loosely with greaseproof paper. Surround the mould with boiling water. Cook the pudding for 50 minutes to 1 hour until just set in the centre.

5 Remove the mould from the baking tin, leave to stand for a few minutes, then turn onto a warmed plate and cover the mould with a damp cloth. Leave for 5 minutes, then remove the mould from the pudding. Serve warm with a little cold Custard or vanilla dairy ice cream.

CRUNCHY MARMALADE PUDDING

SERVES 6–8

This pudding combines several features that make it interesting and enjoyable to eat – a nutty-crunchy top, a sweet tang and appetite-tickling spices. One day when I had a bottle of Guinness open, I substituted it for the milk and was sufficiently pleased with the result that, if I am in the mood for drinking the rest of the bottle, I will open one specifically to make the pudding.

- 4 CLOVES OR A PINCH OF GROUND CLOVES
- 2.5 CM/1 INCH CINNAMON STICK OR 1 TSP GROUND CINNAMON
- 150 G/5 OZ DARK, THICK-CUT MARMALADE, SUCH AS OXFORD, CHOPPED
- 125 G/4½ OZ UNSALTED BUTTER, DICED
- 7 TBSP GOLDEN SYRUP
- 2 EGGS, SIZE 3, BEATEN
- 225 G/8 OZ SELF-RAISING FLOUR
- 1 TSP BAKING POWDER
- ¾ TSP FRESHLY GRATED NUTMEG
- APPROXIMATELY 70 ML/ 2½ FL OZ MILK OR GUINNESS
- 40 G/1½ OZ CORNFLAKES, FINELY CRUSHED
- 40 G/1½ OZ WALNUT HALVES, FINELY CHOPPED
- **TO SERVE:**
- CUSTARD (SEE PAGE 181)

1 Use a pestle and mortar to finely crush the cloves and cinnamon.

2 Set the oven to 180°C/350°F/Gas 4. Butter a 20 cm/8 inch square cake tin and spread 2 tablespoons of the marmalade over the base.

3 Beat the butter with 4½ tablespoons of the syrup until well mixed, then gradually beat in the eggs, keeping the mixture smooth. Stir in half the remaining marmalade.

4 Sift together the flour, baking powder and nutmeg (and cloves and cinnamon if using ready ground ones), then fold into the syrup mixture with the finely crushed cinnamon and cloves. Add sufficient milk or Guinness to make a fairly stiff consistency. Spoon into the dish.

5 Mix the cornflakes and walnuts with the remaining syrup and marmalade, then spread evenly over the pudding. Bake for about 45 minutes until a skewer inserted in the centre comes out clean. Serve hot with plenty of Custard.

Use a pestle in a mortar to crush cinnamon and cloves

PECAN WHISKY PUDDING

SERVES 6

Opinions vary about the sauce for this pudding. Some say that the sweet richness of the sauce complements the opulent nuts, moist raisins and delicate crumb and flavour of the pudding. Others think that it detracts from the pudding's merits, and prefer vanilla dairy ice cream or Iced Mascarpone (see page 80), perhaps laced with a little whisky. The only debate about the pudding itself is how soon will it be served again!

- 125 G/4½ OZ PLUMP RAISINS
- 70 ML/2½ FL OZ WHISKY
- 70 G/2½ OZ UNSALTED BUTTER, DICED
- 85 G/3 OZ LIGHT MUSCOVADO SUGAR
- 2 EGGS, SEPARATED
- 160 G/5¼ OZ PLAIN FLOUR
- 1½ TSP BAKING POWDER
- ½ TSP FRESHLY GRATED NUTMEG
- 150 G/5 OZ PECAN HALVES
- **SAUCE (OPTIONAL):**
- 115 G/4 OZ LIGHT MUSCOVADO SUGAR
- 115 G/4 OZ UNSALTED BUTTER, CHOPPED
- 150 ML/5 FL OZ WHIPPING CREAM
- 1 TSP VANILLA ESSENCE

1 Leave the raisins to soak in the whisky for several hours.

2 Set the oven to 170°C/325°F/Gas 3. Butter and lightly flour a 15 cm/6 inch round baking dish or cake tin.

3 Beat the butter and 100 g/3½ oz of the sugar until light and fluffy, then beat in the egg yolks.

4 Sift together the flour, baking powder and nutmeg. Using a large metal spoon, gently fold into the butter mixture with the nuts and raisins and whisky.

5 In a clean, dry bowl, whisk the egg whites until soft peaks form, then gradually whisk in the remaining sugar. Gently fold half into the egg mixture, then gently fold in the remainder. Spoon into the dish or tin and bake for about 50 minutes until a fine skewer inserted into the centre comes out clean.

6 To make the sauce, if using, gently heat all the ingredients together in a small, heavy-based saucepan, stirring with a wooden spoon, until evenly blended. Remove from the heat and whisk for 1 minute.

7 Leave the cake to cool in the tin or dish for a few minutes, then turn onto a warm plate. Trickle the sauce over. Serve warm.

Illustrated opposite page 64

APRICOT PANDOWDY

SERVES 4 – 6

A pandowdy is an American name for a type of upside-down pudding. The recipe for this version was given to me – after I had eaten two helpings of the pudding – by a friend who has an American aunt who had given it to her.

- 350 G/12 OZ FRESH APRICOTS, HALVED AND STONED
- 85 G/3 OZ SUGAR
- 150 ML/5 FL OZ WATER
- 4 TBSP MAPLE SYRUP
- 55 G/2 OZ UNSALTED BUTTER
- SQUEEZE OF LEMON JUICE
- 55 G/2 OZ PECAN OR WALNUT HALVES
- **TOPPING:**
- 200 G/7 OZ SELF-RAISING FLOUR
- 2 TSP BAKING POWDER
- 100 G/3½ OZ VANILLA SUGAR
- FINELY GRATED RIND AND JUICE OF 1 LEMON
- 115 G/4 OZ UNSALTED BUTTER, DICED
- 115 ML/4 FL OZ BUTTERMILK OR MILK
- 2 EGGS
- **TO SERVE:**
- DOUBLE CREAM, CUSTARD (SEE PAGE 181) OR VANILLA DAIRY ICE CREAM

1 Butter the sides of a 22.5 cm/9 inch cake tin, preferably springform. Set the oven to 180°C/350°F/Gas 4.

2 Put the apricots, sugar and water into a wide saucepan. Heat gently until the sugar dissolves, then cook gently until the apricots are almost tender, about 5 minutes. Drain off and reserve the syrup.

3 Beat the maple syrup with the butter and a squeeze of lemon juice, then spread over the base of the cake tin. Arrange the apricot halves, cut side uppermost, on the base and fill the spaces between them with the pecan or walnut halves.

4 To make the topping, sift the flour and baking powder into a bowl and stir in the vanilla sugar and lemon rind. In a small saucepan, gently heat the butter in the buttermilk until the butter has melted. Remove from the heat, beat in the eggs, then slowly pour onto the flour mixture, stirring constantly to make a smooth batter. Spoon into the tin, taking care not to dislodge the fruit.

5 Bake for about 45 minutes, until a fine skewer inserted in the centre of the topping comes out clean.

6 Just before the pudding is cooked, boil the reserved apricot juice and the lemon juice until reduced by half. Quickly pierce the pudding several times with a fork and pour the very hot syrup over. Turn onto a warmed plate. Serve with cream, Custard or vanilla dairy ice cream.

Illustrated opposite page 32

Spread the cake with the damsons, then roll up from the short end

DAMSON ROLL

SERVES 4

The full, sharp flavour of damsons and the sweet, moist spiciness of the roll are an excellent partnership, which is further enhanced by serving with cool whipped cream or crème fraîche *or strained Greek yogurt.*

- **SPICED ROLL:**
- 115 G/4 OZ PLAIN FLOUR
- 1 TSP BICARBONATE OF SODA
- 1 TSP MIXED SPICE
- 1 TSP VERY FINELY CHOPPED FRESH ROOT GINGER
- 70 G/2½ OZ UNSALTED BUTTER, DICED
- 2 TBSP GOLDEN SYRUP
- 2 TBSP BLACK TREACLE
- 1 EGG, BEATEN
- 150 ML/5 FL OZ SWEET WHITE WINE OR WATER
- CASTER SUGAR, FOR SPRINKLING
- **FILLING:**
- 900 G/2 LB DAMSONS, HALVED AND STONED
- 55 G/2 OZ SUGAR

1 Set the oven to 180°C/350°F/Gas 4. Butter a Swiss roll tin, then line the base with greaseproof paper and butter the paper.

2 To make the filling, gently cook the damsons with the sugar in a covered saucepan until the juices run. Using a slotted spoon, transfer the damsons to a non-metallic sieve and press them through. Leave to cool.

3 To make the spiced roll, stir the flour, bicarbonate of soda and spices together. Form a well in the centre.

4 Gently heat together the butter, syrup and treacle until evenly mixed. Stir in the egg and wine or water. Slowly pour into the well in the spiced flour, gradually drawing the flour into the liquid using a balloon whisk.

5 Beat until smooth, then pour into the tin and sprinkle with a fine layer of caster sugar. Bake for 12–15 minutes until springy to the touch.

6 Sprinkle a sheet of greaseproof paper with caster sugar. Turn the spiced roll onto the paper and carefully peel off the lining. Quickly spread the damsons over the cake. Starting at a narrow end, roll up like a Swiss roll and serve warm.

PARKIN PUDDING

SERVES 6–8

A real winter pudding – lightly sticky and chewy, and slightly spicy, which is offset by the contrasting texture and juicy fruitiness of the pineapple. Use fresh pineapple if possible, otherwise use pineapple canned in natural juice.

- 175 G/6 OZ UNSALTED BUTTER, DICED
- 115 G/4 OZ LIGHT MUSCOVADO SUGAR
- 85 G/3 OZ GOLDEN SYRUP
- 55 G/2 OZ BLACK TREACLE
- 85 ML/3 FL OZ SOURED CREAM
- 175 G/6 OZ PLAIN FLOUR
- 1½ TSP BICARBONATE OF SODA
- 175 G/6 OZ PORRIDGE OATS
- 2 TSP GRATED FRESH ROOT GINGER
- 350–400 G/12–14 OZ PREPARED FRESH, OR DRAINED, CANNED, PINEAPPLE SLICES OR RINGS
- **TO SERVE:**
- VANILLA DAIRY ICE CREAM OR STRAINED GREEK YOGURT

1 Set the oven to 160°C/325°F/Gas 3. Butter a 20 × 12.5 cm/8 × 5 inch oval baking dish, being particularly generous with the butter in the bottom of the dish.

2 Gently heat together the butter, half of the sugar, the syrup, treacle and soured cream, stirring occasionally, until the butter has melted and the sugar dissolved. Remove from the heat, then stir in the flour, bicarbonate of soda, oats and ginger.

3 Put an even layer of pineapple in the pie dish, sprinkle with the remaining sugar, then top with the parkin mixture. Bake for about 1 hour until dark brown and just set in the centre – I think this pudding is better if it is still nice and moist.

4 Run a knife around the edge of the pudding, leave for a couple of minutes, then turn the pudding onto a warmed plate and serve hot with vanilla dairy ice cream or strained Greek yogurt.

HOT BROWNIE SOUFFLÉ WITH ICE CREAM SAUCE

SERVES 4

There are very few children who do not love brownies, and few of them lose the taste when they grow up, so this pudding will appeal to adults and youngsters alike, especially accompanied by the ice cream sauce. When serving it to grown-ups, you could dissolve the coffee in 1 tablespoon of rum or a coffee or orange liqueur.

- 85 G/3 OZ UNSALTED BUTTER
- CASTER SUGAR, FOR SPRINKLING
- 85 G/3 OZ PLAIN CHOCOLATE, CHOPPED
- 100 G/3½ OZ LIGHT MUSCOVADO SUGAR
- 3 EGG YOLKS
- 2 TSP INSTANT COFFEE POWDER
- ¾ TSP VANILLA ESSENCE
- 40 G/1½ OZ SELF-RAISING FLOUR
- 4 EGG WHITES
- **ICE CREAM SAUCE:**
- 425 ML/15 FL OZ VANILLA DAIRY ICE CREAM
- 1½ TSP DARK RUM

1 Set the oven to 230°C/450°F/Gas 8. Butter a 1 litre/1¾ pint soufflé dish and sprinkle the inside lightly with caster sugar.

2 In a bowl, combine the butter and chocolate, place over a saucepan of hot water, and stir occasionally until smooth. Stir in half of the sugar, egg yolks, coffee, vanilla essence and flour. Remove the bowl from the saucepan.

3 In a clean, dry bowl, whisk the egg whites until soft peaks form, then gradually whisk in the remaining sugar until stiff.

4 Using a large metal spoon, gently fold a quarter of the whites into the chocolate mixture, then gently fold the chocolate into the remaining whites. Spoon into the dish, sprinkle a little caster sugar over the top and bake for 5 minutes.

5 Lower the oven temperature to 200°C/400°F/Gas 6 and bake for about 20 minutes until well risen (the centre will still be moist).

6 While the pudding is cooking, place the ice cream for the sauce in a bowl and leave at room temperature for 10 minutes. Beat in the rum, if using, until smooth.

7 Serve the pudding as soon as it is cooked, accompanied by the sauce.

RIGHT (from top to bottom): A Plum Pudding (see page 22); Mother's Mincemeat Pudding (see page 40); Hot Brownie Soufflé with Ice Cream Sauce

CHERRY CASKET

SERVES 4–6

As the name suggests, the filling is enclosed so that when the pudding has been assembled it looks like a plain sponge. Inside though, there is a flavourful cherry compote, which oozes onto the plate when the restraining wall is cut.

- 2 EGGS, SIZE 2, BEATEN
- 115 G/4 OZ VANILLA CASTER SUGAR
- 115 G/4 OZ SELF-RAISING FLOUR
- 115 G/4 OZ UNSALTED BUTTER, MELTED AND COOLED
- FEW DROPS ROSE WATER OR ALMOND ESSENCE (OPTIONAL)
- ICING SUGAR, FOR DUSTING

CHERRY COMPOTE:

- 450 G/1 LB RIPE BLACK CHERRIES, STONED
- 40 G/1 ½ OZ UNSALTED BUTTER
- 2 TSP VANILLA CASTER SUGAR
- PINCH OF GROUND CINNAMON
- JUICE OF 1 ORANGE
- JUICE OF 1 LEMON
- 1–2 TBSP REDCURRANT JELLY
- 2 TBSP KIRSCH OR BRANDY

TO SERVE:

- SABAYON SAUCE (SEE PAGE 185)

1 Set the oven to 190°C/375°F/Gas 5. Butter a 850–1.2 litre/1½–2 pint soufflé dish.

2 Whisk the eggs and sugar together until very thick and pale. Sift the flour over the surface, then, using a large metal spoon, begin to gently fold in, at the same time slowly pouring the butter around the insides of the bowl. Add rose water or almond essence, if liked. Transfer to the dish and bake for about 40–45 minutes until lightly browned and a skewer comes out clean when inserted in the centre.

3 To make the cherry compote, place the cherries in a heavy-based saucepan together with the butter, sugar, cinnamon and orange and lemon juices and heat gently, shaking the pan occasionally, for 5–10 minutes. Drain the cherries, catching the juice. Return the juice to the pan and boil until syrupy. Lower the heat and stir in the redcurrant jelly and kirsch or brandy. Return the cherries to the pan, taste and adjust the sweetness by adding more redcurrant jelly or lemon juice. Cover and keep warm over a very low heat (a diffuser mat might be necessary if using a gas hob).

4 Remove the sponge from the oven, leave for 2–3 minutes, then turn onto a wire rack lined with a tea towel to protect the cake from being marked by the wires. Using a long, sharp knife, cut a thin slice from the uppermost side of the sponge and reserve. Using a large metal spoon, scoop out the centre of the cake to leave a shell with walls approximately 2 cm/¾ inch thick.

5 Spoon the cherry mixture into the sponge then replace the slice. Sift icing sugar over the top and serve immediately with the warm Sabayon Sauce.

LEFT (from top to bottom): Baked Apples with a Middle Eastern Flavour (see page 41); Cherry Casket.

JAQUI'S BREAD AND BUTTER PUDDING

SERVES 4–6

Jaqui, a friend of mine, is very fond of puddings, but her husband, Frank, adores them, or, more particularly, traditional puddings, including bread and butter pudding. This has recently become one of the most fashionable traditional puddings, and many variations have appeared. This one, which is given a refreshing lift by citrus juices and tangy marmalade, pleases Frank and everyone else to whom Jaqui has served it, including me, because it is slightly different without deviating too far from the original and becoming gimmicky.

- 100 G/3½ OZ UNSALTED BUTTER
- 8 THIN SLICES BREAD FROM A SMALL LOAF, 6 FROM A LARGE ONE
- 3½ TBSP BITTER MARMALADE
- FINELY GRATED RIND AND JUICE OF 2 ORANGES
- FINELY GRATED RIND AND JUICE OF 1 LEMON
- 85 G/3 OZ VANILLA CASTER SUGAR
- 425 ML/15 FL OZ MILK
- 3 EGGS, SIZE 3

1 Set the oven to 180°C/350°F/Gas 4. Butter a 1.2 litre/2 pint ovenproof dish.

2 Butter one side of each slice of bread and spread with marmalade. Cut off the crusts and cut each slice into triangles or fingers.

3 In a shallow dish, stir together the orange and lemon rinds and juices and 2 tablespoons of the sugar. Dip the bread in this mixture, then line the bottom and sides of the ovenproof dish with some of the bread. Reserve the remaining orange and lemon mixture and bread.

4 Heat the milk to boiling point in a heavy-based saucepan. In a medium-sized bowl, whisk together the eggs and remaining sugar, then slowly stir in the milk. Pour back into the saucepan and cook over a very low heat, stirring constantly with a wooden spoon until lightly thickened; do not allow to boil.

5 Pour into the dish. Arrange the remaining bread on top, pour over the remaining orange and lemon mixture and bake for about 30–40 minutes until softly set and creamy inside and crisp and golden on top.

VARIATION:
Much to his regret, Frank is unable to eat cream, so Jaqui uses only milk to make the custard, but for a richer pudding you could replace 150 ml/5 fl oz of the milk with the same amount of single, whipping or double cream.

Illustrated opposite page 32

LIGHT APPLE PUDDING

SERVES 4

This recipe started life as Eve's Pudding, or Temptation, a simple creamed sponge mixture baked over apples (hence the name, or so I read), but I have modified it a number of times until this light version, deliciously flavoured with aromatic, sweet but sharp guava, was reached. Guavas combine well with apples and really do give the pudding a special quality, but if they are not available the segments of 2 oranges and 2 tablespoons of demerara sugar, or 55–85 g/2–3 oz dark, chunky marmalade can be substituted for the guava and added to the apples after they have been cooked.

- 1 GUAVA
- COOKING APPLES TO MAKE THE WEIGHT WITH THE GUAVA UP TO 550–700 G/1 ¼–1 ½ LB
- 115 G/4 OZ UNSALTED BUTTER
- APPROXIMATELY 2 TBSP CLEAR HONEY OR SUGAR TO TASTE (OPTIONAL)
- 70 G/2 ½ OZ LIGHT MUSCOVADO SUGAR
- 2 EGGS, SIZE 2, SEPARATED
- 85 G/3 OZ FRESH BREADCRUMBS
- 25 G/1 OZ SELF-RAISING FLOUR

1 Set the oven to 180°C/350°F/Gas 4. Butter a 900 ml/2 pint ovenproof pie dish.

2 Halve the guava, then scoop out and discard the seeds. Core and slice the apples. Heat 25 g/1 oz butter in a saucepan, add the apples, then scoop the flesh from the guava into the pan and cook gently for about 5 minutes; the apple slices should not break up. Remove from the heat and stir in the honey or sugar, if liked. Spoon into the dish to make an even layer.

3 Beat the remaining butter and 55 g/2 oz of the light muscovado sugar together until light and creamy. Gradually beat in the egg yolks.

4 Mix together the breadcrumbs and flour. In a clean bowl, whisk the egg whites until stiff but not dry, then whisk in the remaining sugar. Using a large metal spoon, gently fold one quarter of the egg whites into the creamed mixture. When just evenly combined, add the remaining egg whites in three batches with the dry ingredients.

5 Spoon over the fruit, then bake for about 35 minutes until risen, just set in the centre and golden.

VARIATION:

Use 55 g/2 oz ground almonds or hazelnuts in place of the flour, or 115 g/4 oz in place of both the flour and breadcrumbs, and sprinkle the top with flaked almonds if adding ground almonds.

Illustrated opposite page 17

Quick, Good Pud

SERVES 4

The friend who gave me this recipe said that it served one – herself! A good testimonial to its irresistibility, yet it is very simple to make and uses straightforward store-cupboard ingredients.

- 85 G/3 OZ UNSALTED BUTTER
- 70 G/2½ OZ LIGHT MUSCOVADO SUGAR
- 2 EGGS, SIZE 3, SEPARATED
- 85 G/3 OZ DRIED APRICOTS, CHOPPED, SOAKED OVERNIGHT AND DRAINED
- 55 G/2 OZ HAZELNUTS, CHOPPED
- 85 G/3 OZ PLAIN CAKE CRUMBS

1 Set the oven to 180°C/350°F/Gas 4. Butter an approximately 18 cm/7¼ inch deep round baking dish.

2 Beat the butter and sugar together until light and fluffy, then beat in the egg yolks one at a time.

3 In a clean, dry bowl, whisk the egg whites until stiff but not dry. Using a large metal spoon, fold into the egg yolk mixture in three batches, adding the apricots, hazelnuts and cake crumbs with the final batch.

4 Spoon into the dish and bake for 30 minutes until risen, golden brown and just set in the centre.

CHARLIE'S APPLE DAPPY

SERVES 6

Charlie is a neighbour in the country with whom I trade in the old-fashioned way – for example, in exchange for his runner beans, which put the majority of haricots verts to shame, and armfuls of colourful, fragrant sweet peas, all of which bring more than a hint of the sights and smells of a country garden to a London flat, I share with him what I cook. When prompted into telling me what were his favourites he gave this pudding the highest score of ten out of ten.

- 225 G/8 OZ SELF-RAISING FLOUR
- 1 TSP BAKING POWDER
- 1 TSP MIXED SPICE
- 85 G/3 OZ UNSALTED BUTTER, DICED
- 115 ML/4 FL OZ MILK
- 225 G/8 OZ COOKING APPLES
- 85 G/3 OZ DRIED FIGS, FINELY CHOPPED
- 1 TBSP LIGHT MUSCOVADO SUGAR

SYRUP:

- FINELY GRATED RIND AND JUICE OF 1 LEMON
- 85 G/3 OZ SUGAR
- 85 ML/3 FL OZ WATER
- 15 G/½ OZ UNSALTED BUTTER

TO SERVE:

- CUSTARD (SEE PAGE 181)

1 Set the oven to 180°C/350°F/Gas 4. Butter a shallow ovenproof dish approximately 35 × 17.5 cm/14 × 7 inches.

2 Sift the flour, baking powder and mixed spice into a bowl. Toss in the butter, then rub in until the mixture resembles breadcrumbs. Slowly pour in the milk and quickly mix the ingredients to a soft but not sticky dough using a round-bladed knife.

3 Turn the dough onto a lightly floured surface, knead briefly then roll out to a 27.5 × 25 cm/13 × 10 inch rectangle.

4 Peel, core and grate the apples, toss with the figs, then spread over the dough, leaving a narrow border free around the edge. Roll up the dough like a Swiss roll. Using a large sharp knife, cut the roll into 12 slices and arrange in the dish, cut side uppermost.

5 To make the syrup, gently heat the lemon rind and juice, sugar and water in a small saucepan, stirring with a wooden spoon, until the sugar has dissolved. Bring to the boil, remove from the heat and add the butter. Pour over the slices, sprinkle with the muscovado sugar and bake for 30 minutes. Serve hot with Custard.

Illustrated opposite page 33

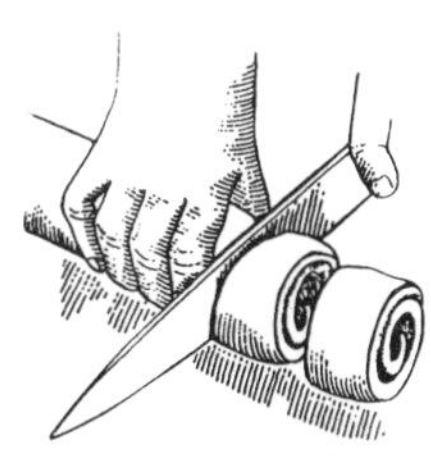

Using a large sharp knife, cut the roll into slices

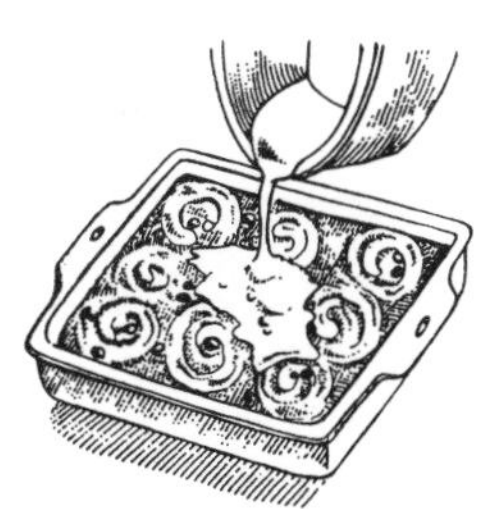

Pour the syrup evenly over the slices in the baking dish

STEAMED PUDDINGS

CHAPTER TWO

Warming, comforting and nostalgic, steamed puddings have a special place in any true pudding-lover's heart. Traditionally, they were served as filling food for hearty appetites in cold weather, but a well-made steamed pudding is not stodgy and heavy, sitting stubbornly in the stomach for what seems like an age afterwards. It can, in fact, be delicate and airy, such as the Light Lemon Pudding, but even the more substantial recipes, such as Marmalade Duff, are just that, more substantial, not leaden. This type of steamed pudding does not have to be reserved for the coldest of winter days and the sharpest of appetites; it can be equally enjoyed at other times – just serve smaller portions.

A steaming basket is useful for cooking steamed puddings, but it is not essential. You can improvise by placing a trivet or an upturned heatproof saucer or small dish in the bottom of a large saucepan and standing the pudding container on it.

STEAMED PUDDINGS

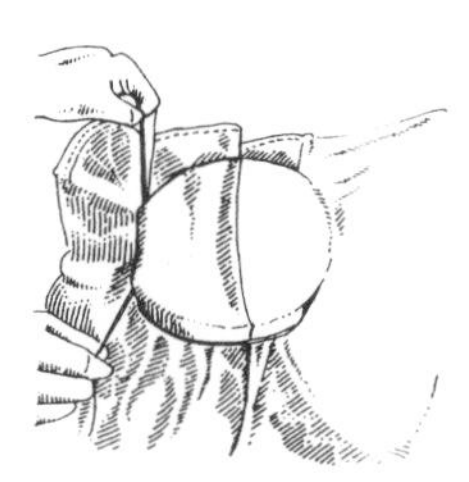

Cover the top of the basin with a cloth pleated across the centre, and tie securely in place with string

Knot the corners of the cloth over the basin. The knot can be used as a handle to lift the pudding

STEAMING TECHNIQUES

☞ A heatproof basin is the most usual container in which to steam a pudding, but other containers, such as brioche or springform cake tins, or individual ramekin dishes, can also be used.

☞ Whether cooking the pudding in a steaming basket or directly in the saucepan, there should be at least a 2.5 cm/1 inch space between the sides of the container and the saucepan or steaming basket to allow steam to circulate.

☞ Fill the saucepan about three-quarters full with water and bring to the boil before starting to prepare the pudding mixture.

☞ Butter the basin or container, then, if possible, place a circle of buttered greaseproof paper in the bottom so that the pudding will turn out easily.

☞ Do not fill the container for the pudding more than two-thirds full with the pudding mixture to allow room for expansion.

☞ To prevent the top of the pudding becoming soggy, butter a piece of greaseproof paper, fold a pleat across the centre so that the pudding can rise, then place the paper over the top of the container. Cover with a piece of foil pleated in the same way, or a pudding-cloth if using a basin with a lip. Secure the paper and foil or cloth by tying string under the lip of the basin. If using a container without a lip, fold the foil and paper under each other around the top of the basin or container. Form a string handle so you can lift the basin or container into and from the saucepan or steaming basket. Alternatively, make a sling from a double thickness of foil and place under the basin or container.

☞ If cooking the pudding in the saucepan rather than in a basket, the water should come about halfway up the sides of the container.

☞ Make sure the water is boiling before starting to cook the pudding, and that it continues to boil throughout the cooking. Keep an eye on the water level and top up with boiling water if necessary.

☞ Cover the top of the steamer or the saucepan with a tight-fitting lid.

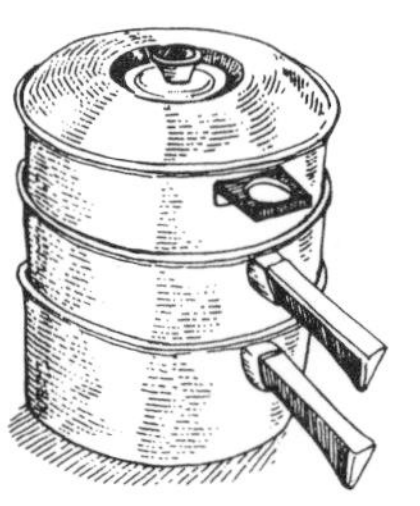

Steamer

Brioche tin

Small heatproof dishes

Cooking steamed puddings in a pressure cooker

Using a pressure cooker can reduce the steaming time by about a third.

☞ The container for the pudding must be able to withstand the higher temperature inside a pressure cooker.

☞ There must be at least 850 ml/1½ pints of water in the cooker.

☞ Before bringing the cooker up to pressure, the pudding must be pre-steamed in boiling water in the pressure cooker with the lid closed but without the weights in place.

☞ Large puddings are usually steamed at LOW (5 lb) pressure, small and individual ones at HIGH (15 lb) pressure.

☞ Release the pressure slowly at the end of the cooking time, following the manufacturer's instructions.

CUMBERLAND RUM PUDDING

SERVES 6

When the pudding is unmoulded, it looks innocuous and not particularly interesting, but secreted in the centre is a wonderful, fragrant moist filling that oozes out as the pudding is cut.

- 175 G/6 OZ UNSALTED BUTTER, DICED
- 350 G/12 OZ PLAIN FLOUR
- 1 TSP BAKING POWDER
- 100 G/3½ OZ LIGHT MUSCOVADO SUGAR
- 1 EGG, BEATEN
- 4 TBSP MILK
- FEW DROPS VANILLA ESSENCE

FILLING:

- 85 G/3 OZ PLUMP RAISINS
- 25 G/1 OZ CANDIED PEEL
- 2 TBSP RUM
- 55 G/2 OZ UNSALTED BUTTER, SOFTENED
- 70 G/2½ OZ LIGHT MUSCOVADO SUGAR
- ½ TSP GROUND CINNAMON

1 Leave the raisins and peel for the filling to soak in the rum for several hours.

2 Butter a 1.2 litre/2 pint pudding basin. Fill a large saucepan three-quarters full with boiling water, place over a high heat and return to the boil.

3 Rub the butter into the flour and baking powder until the mixture resembles breadcrumbs, then stir in the sugar, egg, milk and vanilla essence.

4 Place two-thirds of the mixture in the basin. With the back of a spoon, spread evenly over the base and sides to within 5 cm/2 inches of the top.

5 Beat all the filling ingredients together until well blended. Spoon into the basin. Cover with the remaining pudding mixture, cover the basin and steam (see page 58) for about 1½–1¾ hours until the pudding feels springy to the touch.

6 Turn out onto a warmed serving plate.

Illustrated opposite page 65

COCONUT AND MANDARIN PUDDING

SERVES 4–5

With juicy pieces of mandarin speckled through a unique light-textured and moist, not-too-sweet coconut mixture that is given an extra fillip by an intriguing, subtle hint of aniseed, this recipe never fails to win converts to puddings.

- 85 G/3 OZ DESICCATED COCONUT
- 115 ML/4 FL OZ MILK
- 100 G/3½ OZ UNSALTED BUTTER, DICED
- 70 G/2½ OZ CASTER SUGAR
- 2 EGGS, SIZE 2, SEPARATED
- FEW DROPS VANILLA ESSENCE
- FINELY GRATED RIND OF 1 ORANGE
- 150 G/5 OZ PLAIN FLOUR
- 2 TSP BAKING POWDER
- ½ TSP ANISEEDS, FINELY CRUSHED
- 1 × 200 G/7 OZ CAN MANDARINS, WELL DRAINED AND ROUGHLY CHOPPED
- **TO SERVE:**
- ORANGE CUSTARD (SEE PAGE 182)

1 Fill a large saucepan three-quarters full with boiling water, place over a high heat and return to the boil. Butter a 1.2 litre/2 pint round baking dish.

2 In a medium-sized bowl, stir together the coconut and milk.

3 Beat the butter and sugar together until light and creamy, then gradually beat in the egg yolks and vanilla essence. Add the orange rind.

4 Sift the flour and baking powder together. In a clean, dry bowl, whisk the egg whites until stiff but not dry, then, using a large metal spoon, gently fold into the creamed mixture in batches alternating with the flour mixture and aniseeds. Lightly fold in the coconut and mandarins.

5 Transfer the mixture to the dish, cover the top of the dish and steam (see page 58) for about 2¾ hours until lightly set. Remove from the heat and serve with Orange Custard.

Illustrated opposite page 16

Making glazed lemon rind:

Pare strips of rind from the lemon, taking care not to include any white pith

Pile the strips on top of each other, then cut into fine shreds, using a large sharp knife

Add fine shreds of blanched citrus rind to a light sugar and water syrup.

LIGHT LEMON PUDDING

SERVES 4

One taste of this pudding with its fresh flavour and feather-light texture will quickly dispel the lie that steamed puddings are heavy and to be avoided at all costs. It takes someone with a lot of willpower to resist a second mouthful.

- 2 TBSP LEMON CURD
- 115 G/4 OZ UNSALTED BUTTER
- 115–150 G/4–5 OZ SUGAR
- 2 EGGS, SEPARATED
- 55 G/2 OZ SELF-RAISING FLOUR
- 55 G/2 OZ FRESH BREADCRUMBS
- JUICE AND FINELY GRATED RIND OF 2 LEMONS

- **LEMON SAUCE:**
- JUICE AND GRATED RIND OF 3 LARGE, JUICY LEMONS
- 1 ROUNDED TSP ARROWROOT
- APPROXIMATELY 85 G/3 OZ CASTER SUGAR
- 85 G/3 OZ UNSALTED BUTTER, DICED
- **DECORATION:**
- GLAZED LEMON RIND (SEE NOTE)

1 Butter a 850 ml/1½ pint pudding basin, then coat the base and inside with lemon curd. Prepare a steamer.

2 Beat together the butter and sugar until light and creamy, then gradually beat in the egg yolks. Using a large metal spoon, lightly fold in the flour, breadcrumbs and lemon juice and rind.

3 In a clean, dry bowl, whisk the egg whites until stiff but not dry, then gently fold into the lemon mixture using the metal spoon. Spoon into the basin, cover (see page 58) and steam for about 1½ hours.

4 To make the sauce, in a small bowl mix a little lemon juice with the arrowroot. Put the arrowroot mixture, the sugar and butter into a saucepan and heat, stirring, until smooth, thickened and clear. Adjust the sweetness, if necessary. Turn the pudding onto a warmed serving plate, pour over some of the sauce and sprinkle with glazed lemon rind.

NOTE: To make the glazed lemon rind, pare thin strips of lemon rind, taking care not to include any white pith. Cut into thin strips, then add to a small saucepan of boiling water, and boil for 2 minutes. Drain and refresh under cold running water. Gently heat 25 g/1 oz sugar in 2 tablespoons of water in the saucepan, then add the lemon strips and simmer for 8–10 minutes until transparent. Remove using a slotted spoon. The strips can be kept in an airtight container for 2 days.

Marmalade Duff

SERVES 6

'Duff' signifies a steamed pudding containing suet, the thought of which can make some people's hearts, or stomachs, sink, while other people's eyes light up at the prospect of a good, hearty pudding. This recipe will please both camps. Soft white breadcrumbs lighten the 'duff' mixture and the chunky pieces of bitter marmalade add a welcoming 'bite' and tang. For a final, wicked touch, pour warmed orange juice and whisky over the pudding after turning it out of the basin.

- 115 G/4 OZ SELF-RAISING FLOUR
- 115 G/4 OZ SOFT WHITE BREADCRUMBS
- 25 G/1 OZ DEMERARA SUGAR
- 1 TSP MIXED SPICE
- 115 G/4 OZ SHREDDED SUET
- 175 G/6 OZ CHUNKY, DARK MARMALADE
- MILK OR ORANGE JUICE TO MIX
- **TO SERVE:**
- CUSTARD (SEE PAGE 181)

1 Butter a 1.2 litre/2 pint pudding basin. Fill a large saucepan three-quarters full with boiling water, place over a high heat and return to the boil.

2 Stir together the flour, breadcrumbs, sugar, mixed spice and suet. Stir in the marmalade and sufficient milk or orange juice to give a soft, dropping consistency. Turn into the basin, cover the top of the basin and steam (see page 58) for 2½ hours until the top feels springy to the touch.

3 Turn onto a warmed serving plate and serve with plenty of Custard.

Illustrated opposite page 65

Stem Ginger Pudding with an Orange Cap

SERVES 5–6

Although you might think that turning this pudding out would not make any difference to its enjoyment, the glistening orange cap looks so appetizing and appealing that the taste buds are stimulated and the overall eating experience enhanced.

- 3 TBSP GOLDEN SYRUP, WARMED
- 2 MEDIUM ORANGES
- 115 G/4 OZ UNSALTED BUTTER
- 85 G/3 OZ DEMERARA SUGAR
- 2 EGGS, BEATEN
- 175 G/6 OZ SELF-RAISING FLOUR
- 1 TSP BICARBONATE OF SODA
- 1½ TSP GROUND GINGER
- 6 PIECES PRESERVED STEM GINGER IN SYRUP, DRAINED AND CHOPPED
- 2 TBSP GINGER SYRUP
- MILK (OPTIONAL)
- **TO SERVE:**
- CUSTARD (SEE PAGE 181)

1 Butter a 1.5 litre/2½ pint pudding basin, add the syrup and tilt the basin to coat the sides. Cut each orange into 6 slices, put into a saucepan of cold water and boil for 3 minutes. Using a slotted spoon, transfer to absorbent kitchen paper to drain. Arrange on the bottom and around the sides of the basin. Fill a large saucepan three-quarters full with boiling water, place over a high heat and return to the boil.

2 Beat the butter and sugar together well, then gradually beat in the eggs, adding a tablespoon or so of the flour towards the end. Using a large metal spoon, lightly fold in the flour, bicarbonate of soda, ground ginger and stem ginger, then add the ginger syrup and sufficient milk to make a soft, dropping consistency, if necessary.

3 Spoon into the basin, taking care not to dislodge the orange slices. Cover the basin and steam (see page 58) for about 1½–1¾ hours until the pudding feels springy to the touch.

4 Turn out onto a warmed plate and serve with Custard.

RIGHT (from top to bottom): Blackberry Meringue Shortbread Cake (see page 37); Magic Lime Pudding (see page 27); Pecan Whisky Pudding (see page 44).

FRAGRANT ALMOND SPONGE WITH APRICOT CREAM SAUCE

SERVES 6

The contrast of the cold tang of the sauce with the warm spice of the pudding makes a deliciously enticing combination.

- 100 G/3½ OZ BLANCHED ALMONDS, GROUND
- 175 G/6 OZ UNSALTED BUTTER, SOFTENED
- 85 G/3 OZ VANILLA SUGAR
- 85 G/3 OZ LIGHT MUSCOVADO SUGAR
- SEEDS FROM 4 LARGE GREEN CARDAMOM PODS, CRUSHED
- 3 EGGS, BEATEN
- 100 G/3½ OZ SELF-RAISING FLOUR
- 55 G/2 OZ TOASTED FLAKED ALMONDS
- ICING SUGAR, FOR DUSTING (OPTIONAL)
- **SAUCE:**
- 225 G/8 OZ DRIED APRICOTS, SOAKED OVERNIGHT
- JUICE AND FINELY GRATED RIND OF 1 SMALL ORANGE
- 150 ML/5 FL OZ SOURED CREAM

1 Lightly butter six 150 ml/5 fl oz ramekin dishes, then sprinkle about half a teaspoon of ground almonds into each ramekin, shaking the ramekin to coat the sides and base evenly. Half fill a large saucepan with water and bring to the boil.

2 Beat the butter, sugars and cardamom seeds together until very light and fluffy. Gradually beat in the eggs, beating well after each addition and adding a little of the flour towards the end. Fold in the remaining flour and ground almonds. Spoon into the ramekins. Cover loosely with buttered greaseproof paper, place in a steaming basket, cover and steam (see page 58) for about 40–45 minutes or until a skewer inserted into the centre comes out clean.

3 Meanwhile, make the sauce. Drain the apricots and reserve the soaking liquor. Purée the fruit with the orange rind and the juice made up to 150 ml/5 fl oz with the soaking liquor to give a thick pouring consistency. Add more of the liquor if necessary. Whisk in the soured cream then cover and chill.

4 Turn the ramekins out onto warm plates, spoon some of the sauce onto the centre of each pudding so that it runs down the sides and sprinkle with toasted flaked almonds and dust with icing sugar, if liked.

LEFT (from top to bottom): Fragrant Almond Sponge with Apricot Cream Sauce; Cumberland Rum Pudding (see page 60); Marmalade Duff (see page 63).

Christmas Pudding

SERVES 6 – 8

I think a good Christmas pudding is amongst the best puddings in the world. But, of course, 'good' is the operative word. Too many people have been turned away from Christmas pudding by examples that were heavy and with too high a suet content, but nowadays the move towards better quality, lighter foods made from more 'pure' ingredients means that far superior versions are being made, both at home and commercially. Although the list of ingredients for Christmas pudding is long, the method is short and easy. I admit that the whole process does take a little time, though, as the fruit and pudding benefit from being allowed to soak and the cooking is lengthy, but does that matter? Other advantages of a home-made pudding is that you can make it months in advance so it has time to mature (manufacturers do not do this because it means a 'negative cash flow') and you can make an all-important wish when you stir the pudding.

- 400 G/14 OZ MIXED SULTANAS, CURRANTS AND LARGE, PLUMP RAISINS
- 115 G/4 OZ PRUNES, STONED AND CHOPPED
- 55 G/2 OZ MIXED PEEL, CHOPPED
- 55 G/2 OZ EACH ALMONDS, HAZELNUTS AND BRAZIL NUTS, FINELY CHOPPED
- 200 ML/7 FL OZ GUINNESS
- GRATED RIND AND JUICE OF 1 LEMON
- GRATED RIND AND JUICE OF 1 ORANGE
- 2 TBSP RUM OR BRANDY
- 115 G/4 OZ UNSALTED BUTTER
- 115 G/4 OZ DARK MUSCOVADO SUGAR
- 2 EGGS, BEATEN
- 85 G/3 OZ SELF-RAISING FLOUR
- 150 G/5 OZ FRESH WHITE BREADCRUMBS
- 1 TSP MIXED SPICE
- ¾ TSP GROUND CINNAMON
- ¾ TSP GROUND GINGER
- LARGE PINCH OF GRATED NUTMEG
- 1 DESSERT APPLE, GRATED (PEEL AND ALL)
- 85 G/3 OZ CARROT, GRATED
- 2 TBSP BLACK TREACLE
- **TO SERVE:**
- 4 TBSP BRANDY, TO FLAME
- BRANDY BUTTER SAUCE (SEE PAGE 186)

1 Put the dried fruits, prunes, mixed peel and nuts in a large bowl, pour over the Guinness, orange and lemon juices and brandy or rum, stir well, cover and leave in a cool place, not the refrigerator, overnight.

2 Beat the butter with the sugar until light and fluffy, then gradually beat in the eggs, beating well after each addition. Using a large metal spoon, fold in the flour, breadcrumbs, spices, grated apple and carrot, soaked fruits and nuts and the soaking liquor and black treacle. Cover the bowl and leave in a cool place, not the refrigerator, overnight.

3 Fill a large saucepan three-quarters full with water and bring to the boil. Butter a 1.5–1.6 litre/2½–2¾ pint pudding basin, then line the base with a double thickness of greaseproof paper and butter the paper. Spoon the pudding mixture into the basin, then cover with two circles of greaseproof paper and finally with foil tied securely in place with string. Steam (see page 58) for 8 hours; keep an eye on the level of water in the saucepan and top up as necessary.

4 Leave until cold, then cover with fresh foil and keep in a cold, dry place.

5 To reheat the pudding, steam again for 5 hours. To flame, warm the brandy in a small saucepan, pour over the pudding and set alight using a lighted taper. Carefully baste with the flaming brandy. Serve with Brandy Butter.

Illustrated opposite page 161

HONEY AND CINNAMON PUDDING

SERVES 4

A pudding whose simplicity belies how good it is to eat, with its combination of flavours that is always welcoming and appetizing, and its top and sides bathed in honey.

- 4 TBSP CLEAR HONEY, GENTLY WARMED
- 115 G/4 OZ UNSALTED BUTTER
- 55 G/2 OZ LIGHT MUSCOVADO SUGAR
- 2 EGGS, SIZE 2, BEATEN
- 115 G/4 OZ SELF-RAISING FLOUR
- GRATED RIND OF 1 LEMON
- ¾ TSP GROUND CINNAMON

1 Butter an 850 ml/1½ pint pudding basin, then add the honey and swirl the basin around to coat the sides and base. Fill a large saucepan three-quarters full with water and bring to the boil.

2 Using a wooden spoon, beat the butter and sugar together until light and creamy, then gradually beat in the eggs. Using a large metal spoon, gently fold in the flour, lemon rind and cinnamon. Transfer to the basin, cover the top of the basin and steam (see page 58) for 1½ hours until a skewer inserted into the centre of the pudding comes out clean.

3 Turn onto a warmed serving plate.

STICKY FIG PUDDING

SERVES 6

The quintessential steamed pudding; this is manna to all lovers of good food.

- 150 G/5 OZ DRIED FIGS, CHOPPED
- 150 ML/5 FL OZ BOILING WATER
- 85 G/3 OZ UNSALTED BUTTER, CHOPPED
- 115 G/4 OZ LIGHT MUSCOVADO SUGAR
- 1 EGG, BEATEN
- 175 G/6 OZ PLAIN FLOUR
- 1 TSP BAKING POWDER
- ½ TSP BICARBONATE OF SODA

TOPPING:

- 85 G/3 OZ UNSALTED BUTTER, DICED
- 175 G/6 OZ DARK MUSCOVADO SUGAR
- 3 TBSP DOUBLE CREAM (OPTIONAL)
- 2 TBSP DARK RUM

TO SERVE:

- BRANDY BUTTER SAUCE OR ONE OF THE VARIATIONS (SEE PAGE 186) OR RUM-FLAVOURED CREAM OR BUTTER, OR VANILLA DAIRY ICE CREAM

1 Soak the figs in the boiling water for about 1 hour. Butter a 1.5 litre/2½ pint pudding basin. Fill a large saucepan three-quarters full with boiling water, place over a high heat and return to the boil.

2 Put the topping ingredients except the rum in a small saucepan, then heat gently, stirring occasionally, until the butter has melted and the sugar dissolved. Bring to the boil, then simmer for 3 minutes. Pour into the pudding basin.

3 Beat together the butter and sugar until light and fluffy. Gradually beat in the egg. Sift over the flour, baking powder and bicarbonate of soda, then fold in using a large metal spoon. Fold in the figs and soaking liquid.

4 Transfer to the basin, cover the top of the basin and steam (see page 58) for about 2 hours until the pudding is springy to the touch.

5 Turn the pudding onto a warmed serving plate to serve.

CARROT AND SWEET POTATO PUDDING

SERVES 4

Do try this recipe – it was an experiment that worked extremely well. No one suspects that it is based on anything out-of-the-ordinary as they gobble it up, and being made privy to its components usually provides them with an excuse to ask for second helpings. My reasoning behind the initial experiment was that while sweet carrot cakes and puddings are quite widely well known and popular, sweet potatoes often have an even sweeter taste than carrots and taste good with sugar or honey and in Latin America they are actually used for puddings – so why not combine sweet potatoes and carrots? The two vegetables enhance each other, so the result is better than if either was used alone.

- 1 SWEET POTATO, ABOUT 350 G/12 OZ
- 115 G/4 OZ GRATED CARROTS
- FINELY GRATED RIND AND JUICE OF 1 LARGE ORANGE
- 55 G/2 OZ UNSALTED BUTTER
- 55 G/2 OZ LIGHT MUSCOVADO SUGAR
- 55 G/2 OZ DARK MUSCOVADO SUGAR
- 3 EGGS, SEPARATED
- 85 G/3 OZ SELF-RAISING FLOUR
- 1 TSP BAKING POWDER
- **TO SERVE:**
- APRICOT SAUCE (SEE PAGE 187) OR FLUFFY ORANGE SAUCE (SEE PAGE 184)

1 Set the oven to 180°C/350°F/Gas 4. Prick the sweet potato all over and bake for about 1¼ hours until tender. Peel off the skin, then purée or mash the flesh. Mix with the carrots and the orange rind.

2 Butter a 1.5 litre/2½ pint pudding basin. Half fill a large saucepan with water and bring to the boil.

3 Beat the butter with the sugars, then gradually beat in the egg yolks. Using a large metal spoon, fold in the flour, baking powder and carrot mixture.

4 In a clean, dry bowl, whisk the egg whites until stiff but not dry. Using a large metal spoon, gently fold into the carrot mixture, then spoon into the basin. Cover the top of the basin and steam (see page 58) for about 1¾ hours until a skewer inserted in the centre comes out clean. Serve with Apricot Sauce or Fluffy Orange Sauce.

WHAT WENT WRONG?

☞ THE PUDDING IS HEAVY:
This is caused by insufficient raising agent, whether a chemical one such as baking powder, or air, being used, or the water going off the boil.

☞ THE PUDDING DOES NOT TURN OUT CLEANLY:
The pudding will not turn out cleanly if the container was not buttered, or was not buttered sufficiently.

☞ THE PUDDING IS NOT COOKED IN THE CENTRE:
The cooking time was insufficient or the water was not kept boiling throughout are the causes of this.

FRIED AND OTHER PUDDINGS

Fried puddings, whether a mouthwatering Strawberry Soufflé Omelette (see page 81), crisp Cinnamon Churros (see page 79), or Pear and Ginger Sauté (see page 80), are all cooked quickly and deserve to be eaten piping hot from the pan. This, I think, makes them very sociable puddings that inspire informality.

The remaining entries in this chapter do not fall conveniently into any other categories. I did not see why, however, this should be a reason for excluding some of my favourite recipes. Each dish is an individual, with its own particular method of preparation and cooking. When making the selections, I realized that they are all traditional recipes from various countries around the world, from England across Europe to Thailand. Consequently, they are cooked on the hob, ovens having only relatively recently been in general use in ordinary people's kitchens in the West and not yet having a place in kitchens in the East or even the Middle East.

FRIED AND OTHER PUDDINGS

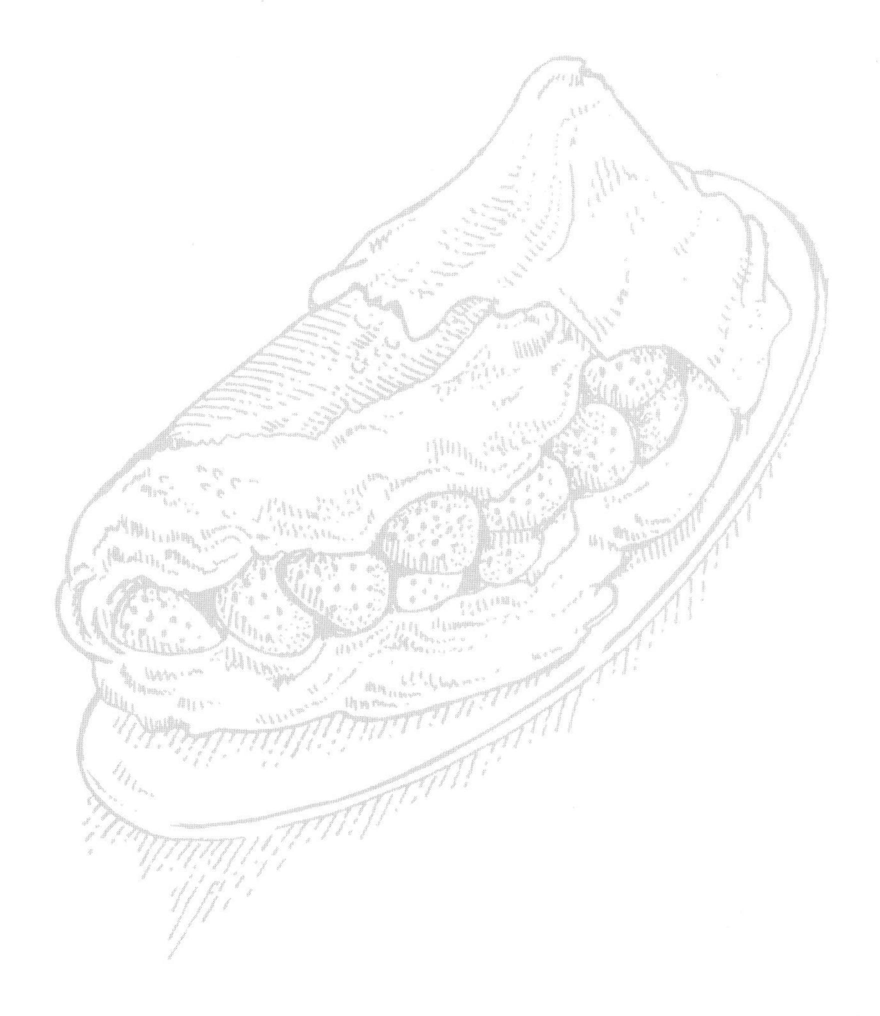

MAPLE SYRUP AND GRAPEFRUIT PANCAKES

SERVES 4

One day when searching for something a little different for a pudding, I tried this recipe although I was a little unsure about how well it would be received. Silence followed serving, which immediately told me that it had met with complete approval. The pancakes are really a cross between conventional pancakes and the thicker drop scones, or pikelets.

BATTER:
- 115 G/4 OZ PLAIN FLOUR
- 1 TSP BAKING POWDER
- ½ TSP GROUND CINNAMON
- 1 TSP CASTER SUGAR
- 1 WHOLE EGG, SIZE 3, BEATEN
- 1 EGG YOLK
- 175 ML/6 FL OZ MILK

TOPPING:
- 3 GRAPEFRUIT
- 6 TBSP MAPLE SYRUP
- 15 G/½ OZ UNSALTED BUTTER, PLUS EXTRA FOR FRYING

TO SERVE:
- VANILLA DAIRY ICE CREAM

1 To make the batter, sift the flour with the baking powder, cinnamon and sugar into a bowl. Form a well in the centre, add the egg and egg yolk and gradually pour in the milk, drawing the dry ingredients into the liquids to make a smooth batter. Leave to stand for 30 minutes.

2 To make the topping, remove the pith and peel from 2 of the grapefruit, then, holding 1 grapefruit over a bowl (to catch any juice), use a small sharp knife to cut down between the flesh and the skin of a segment and remove it. Repeat all the way around the grapefruit, then prepare the other peeled grapefruit in the same way. Squeeze the juice from the third grapefruit and pour into a small saucepan with any juice that has collected in the bowl. Stir in the maple syrup and set to one side.

3 Heat a heavy frying pan, then add a small knob of butter. When it is hot, stir the batter and pour a couple of tablespoonfuls into the pan, spreading the mixture out to a circle approximately 9 cm/3½ inches in diameter. Repeat two or three times more, but do not crowd the pan, and cook over a moderate heat until bubbles appear on the surface, then turn over and cook for a further 2 minutes until lightly browned underneath. Using a fish slice, transfer to a folded tea towel to keep warm while cooking the remaining batter.

4 Bring the grapefruit juice and maple syrup to the boil, lower the heat and swirl in the butter.

5 Serve the pancakes topped with grapefruit segments and spoon the sauce onto the fruit. Serve with vanilla dairy ice cream.

Illustrated opposite page 16

Crema fritta de luxe

SERVES 4–6

Two recipes, one Italian, Crema fritta *(also prepared in Spain and called* Lecha frite*), and one French, for cream cheese* beignets, *have been merged into one and further modifications made to give a luscious, soft, feather-light filling contained in a crisp coating. The custard mixture can be flavoured to taste with a liqueur, brandy, whisky, rum or orange flower water or rose water (do not use lemon cake crumbs if using a flower water).*

- 115 G/4 OZ RICOTTA CHEESE, SIEVED
- APPROXIMATELY 2 TBSP CASTER SUGAR
- 3 EGGS, SIZE 2, BEATEN
- FEW DROPS VANILLA ESSENCE
- 40 G/1½ OZ PLAIN FLOUR
- 200 ML/7 FL OZ WHIPPING CREAM
- 200 ML/7 FL OZ MILK
- 100 G/3½ OZ CAKE CRUMBS, PREFERABLY LEMON
- VEGETABLE OIL FOR DEEP FRYING
- **TO SERVE:**
- FRESH FRUIT SAUCE, SUCH AS FRESH APRICOT, NECTARINE, RASPBERRY OR BLACKCURRANT

1 Lightly flour a baking sheet.

2 In a bowl, beat the cheese with the sugar. Gradually beat in two of the eggs and the vanilla essence, then stir in the flour. Using a balloon whisk, gradually whisk in the cream and milk.

3 Pour into a heavy, preferably non-stick, saucepan and heat gently, stirring, until thickened; do not allow to boil.

4 Pour onto the baking sheet to make an even layer about 1.25 cm/½ inch thick, leave to cool completely, then cover and place in the refrigerator for at least 1 hour.

5 Cut the cold custard mixture into approximately 2.5 cm/1 inch squares, rectangles or diamonds. Dip in the remaining egg, then in the cake crumbs.

6 Half fill a deep-fat frying pan with vegetable oil and heat to 190°C/375°F. Add the coated shapes in batches and cook for about 1½ minutes until golden and crisp on the outside. Keep an eye on the temperature of the oil to make sure that it does not drop; the shapes must cook very quickly. Using a slotted spoon, transfer to absorbent kitchen paper, drain quickly and serve immediately accompanied by a fruit sauce.

Illustrated opposite page 80

Coat shapes in beaten egg, then in crumbs

CARIBBEAN BANANAS

SERVES 4

Orange, lime, allspice, rum and brown sugar all seem to have a natural affinity with bananas and each other, so it is not surprising that when they are all used together the result is a success.

- 4 FIRM BANANAS
- 40 G/1½ OZ UNSALTED BUTTER
- 1 TSP FINELY CRUSHED ALLSPICE BERRIES OR GROUND MIXED SPICE
- 2 TBSP DARK MUSCOVADO SUGAR
- GRATED RIND OF ½ ORANGE
- JUICE OF 1 LARGE ORANGE
- JUICE OF 1 LIME
- 3 TBSP RUM
- 1 TBSP COINTREAU OR OTHER ORANGE LIQUEUR

1 Peel the bananas and cut diagonally into thick slices.

2 Heat the butter in a frying pan, stir in the allspice or mixed spice, then the bananas and fry gently, turning occasionally, until the bananas have softened and are lightly browned. Transfer the bananas to a warmed serving dish.

3 Heat the sugar in the pan until dissolved and lightly caramelized, then stir in the orange rind and juice and the lime juice. Bubble for a few minutes until lightly thickened. Return the bananas to the pan and remove from the heat.

4 Heat the rum and liqueur in a ladle over a flame. Using a lighted taper, ignite the rum and liqueur, then carefully pour into the pan, returning it to the heat and shaking it to mix the ingredients. Serve immediately.

Cinnamon Churros

SERVES 4

In Spain, churros *are eaten, freshly made and piping hot, for breakfast, but they also make a very good pudding. In place of the traditional large cups of rich chocolate that accompany* churros *and are just right for dunking them in, serve with Hot Chocolate Sauce.*

- 100 G/3½ OZ SELF-RAISING FLOUR
- ¼ TSP GROUND CINNAMON
- 55 G/2 OZ UNSALTED BUTTER, DICED
- 185 ML/6½ FL OZ WATER
- 3–4 EGGS, SIZE 2, BEATEN
- VEGETABLE OIL FOR DEEP FRYING

- **TO FINISH:**
- MIXTURE OF VANILLA CASTER SUGAR AND ICING SUGAR, FOR DUSTING
- **TO SERVE:**
- HOT CHOCOLATE SAUCE (SEE PAGE 183)

1 Sift the flour and cinnamon onto a plate and place beside the hob. Gently heat the butter in the water until the butter has melted, then quickly bring to the boil. Immediately remove from the heat and quickly add the flour mixture in one go and beat vigorously until smooth. Return to the heat for about 30 seconds, still beating. Remove from the heat and allow to cool slightly. Gradually beat in the eggs until the mixture is a smooth, thick, glossy paste.

2 Half fill a deep-fat frying pan with oil and heat to 190°C/375°F.

3 Spoon the egg mixture into a piping bag fitted with a 5 mm–1.25 cm/¼–½ inch plain nozzle and pipe lengths into the hot oil, forming them into rings, spirals or horseshoes; use a sharp knife to cut off the mixture at the required length and only cook about three at a time. Fry for about 3–4 minutes, turning once, until golden.

4 Using a slotted spoon, transfer the *churros* to absorbent kitchen paper to drain. Keep warm while frying the remaining mixture. Serve hot, dusted thickly with the sugar mixture, and with the Hot Chocolate Sauce in a jug.

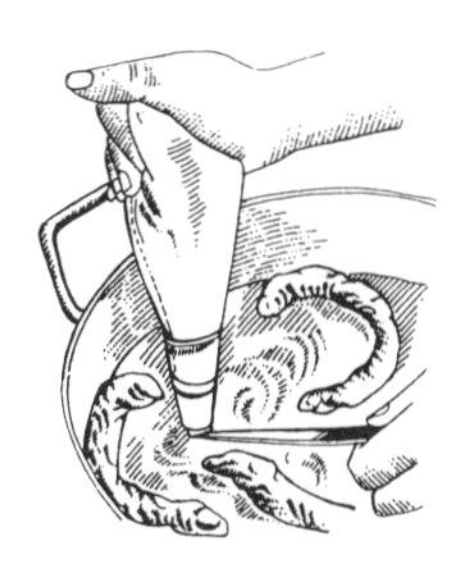

Pipe lengths of dough into the hot oil, cutting the dough off at the required length, near the nozzle

PEAR AND GINGER SAUTÉ WITH ICED MASCARPONE

SERVES 4

Recipes such as this, for puddings that can be made very quickly and are a little out of the ordinary (and, of course, delicious), are always useful to have. The pears with their ginger-spiked sauce are very good as they are, but the smooth richness of the iced mascarpone lifts the dish into a different class, melting deliciously on the pears and into the sauce.

- 4 FIRM BUT RIPE PEARS
- 55 G/2 OZ UNSALTED BUTTER
- ½ TSP GROUND GINGER
- 2 TBSP WALNUT HALVES, ROUGHLY CHOPPED
- 1½ TBSP SYRUP FROM THE JAR OF PRESERVED GINGER
- 2 TBSP DRY WHITE WINE, PREFERABLY MEDIUM-BODIED (OPTIONAL)
- 1 PIECE STEM GINGER, SLICED
- LEMON JUICE
- **ICED MASCARPONE:**
- 2 EGG YOLKS, SIZE 3
- 85 G/3 OZ ICING SUGAR
- 225 G/8 OZ MASCARPONE CHEESE
- FEW DROPS VANILLA ESSENCE

1 To make the iced mascarpone, beat the egg yolks with the icing sugar, then gradually whisk in the mascarpone. Flavour with a few drops of vanilla essence, then spoon into a freezer-proof container. Cover and freeze for at least 6 hours. Return to the refrigerator about 30 mintues before serving.

2 Peel the pears, core and cut each one into quarters.

3 Heat the butter in a frying pan, stir in the ginger, then add the pears and walnuts and cook gently for about 6–8 minutes until the pears are tender; turn them over carefully after about 3 minutes.

4 Stir in the syrup from the ginger jar and the wine, if liked, then allow to bubble until lightly syrupy. Stir in the stem ginger and add a little lemon juice, to 'lift'. Serve straight away with the Iced Mascarpone.

RIGHT (from top to bottom): Pear and Ginger Sauté with Iced Mascarpone ; Crema Fritta de Luxe (see page 77); Strawberry Soufflé Omelette (see page 81).

STRAWBERRY SOUFFLÉ OMELETTE

SERVES 2

This is a delightful pudding. At first glance it may seem a little complicated, but a closer inspection will reveal that it involves no more than a series of simple, short steps and not all the ingredients are essential (although certainly worth including if you can). The purée and the strawberries can also be warmed.

- 225 G/8 OZ STRAWBERRIES
- FINELY GRATED RIND AND JUICE OF 1 ORANGE
- 2 TBSP CASTER SUGAR
- 4 EGGS, SIZE 3
- 150 ML/5 FL OZ MILK
- 1 ALMOND MACAROON, CRUSHED
- 1 TBSP WHIPPING CREAM
- 15 G/½ OZ UNSALTED BUTTER
- 1 TBSP FLAKED ALMONDS (OPTIONAL)
- ICING SUGAR FOR SPRINKLING (OPTIONAL)

1 Cut two-thirds of the strawberries into halves and sprinkle over the orange rind and half the juice. Cover and set aside.

2 Purée the remaining strawberries in a blender or food processor with the remaining orange juice and 1 tablespoon of sugar. Strain the purée through a non-metallic sieve; discard the seeds.

3 In a heatproof medium-sized bowl, placed over a saucepan of hot water, whisk 1 egg with 1½ teaspoons of sugar. Heat the milk to boiling point, then slowly whisk into the egg. Cook, stirring with a wooden spoon, until slightly thickened. Remove the bowl from the pan and leave the custard to cool, stirring occasionally.

4 Separate the remaining eggs. Whisk the yolks with the remaining sugar. In a separate clean, dry bowl, using a clean whisk, lightly fold the macaroon and cream into the egg yolks, then gently fold in the egg whites until just evenly combined.

5 Melt the butter in a 17.5 cm/7 inch omelette pan, add the flaked almonds, if using, fry until lightly browned, then add the egg mixture and cook over a moderate heat until browned underneath and almost set.

6 Slide the omelette onto a warmed serving plate, place the strawberry halves on one half of the omelette and fold it over. Spoon over the strawberry purée and pour the custard over the open edge. Sprinkle with a little icing sugar, if liked.

Illustrated opposite page 80

LEFT (from top to bottom): Dried Fruit Compote (see page 82); Austrian Pillows with Plum and Raspberry Compote (see page 87); Mangoes with Sticky Rice (see page 88).

DRIED FRUIT COMPOTE

SERVES 6

I never tire of dried fruit compote, which can be eaten at any time of the day and night, not just as a pudding. The recipe is enormously variable – apple juice is not necessary, but it really enhances the fruity taste. Orange juice could also be used, in which case I would omit the orange segments. Ginger wine is another option, and all the spices can be changed, in quantity as well as selection. Plenty of chopped fresh ginger stirred in with the oranges is one of my favourite variations. A dried fruit compote is a very useful pudding as it needs very little preparation or cooking. In fact, it can be made without any cooking at all – simply leave the fruits to soak in a covered bowl in the refrigerator for at least 2 days, stirring occasionally. Not only will it stay in good condition (if given a chance!), but it will also improve over a number of days.

- 700 G/1½ LB MIXED DRIED FRUITS SUCH AS PEARS, APRICOTS (PREFERABLY HUNZA), FIGS, PEACHES, PRUNES AND APPLE RINGS
- 1 LEMON
- 2 LARGE ORANGES
- SEEDS FROM 6 GREEN CARDAMOM PODS, LIGHTLY CRUSHED
- 425 ML/15 FL OZ FRUITY MEDIUM DRY WHITE WINE, SUCH AS CHENIN BLANC
- 300 ML/10 FL OZ APPLE JUICE
- 1 CINNAMON STICK ABOUT 5 CM/2 IN LONG
- 4 STAR ANISE PODS (OPTIONAL)
- 4 CLOVES
- **TO SERVE:**
- CHILLED STRAINED GREEK YOGURT

1 Place all the dried fruits in a bowl. Using a potato peeler, pare a long strip of rind from the lemon and one of the oranges. Squeeze the juice from the lemon. Add the juice, citrus peels and spices to the bowl, pour over the wine, stir, cover and leave in a cool place over night.

2 Tip the contents of the bowl into a saucepan, add the apple juice and heat to simmering point, then simmer gently for about 25 minutes until the fruit is just tender – adjust the cooking to suit how soft you like the fruit to be and remember that the fruit will continue to soften as it cools. Leave to cool.

3 Just before serving, peel the orange and divide into segments, removing all the skin and pith, stir into the dried fruits. Serve with strained Greek yogurt.

Illustrated opposite page 81

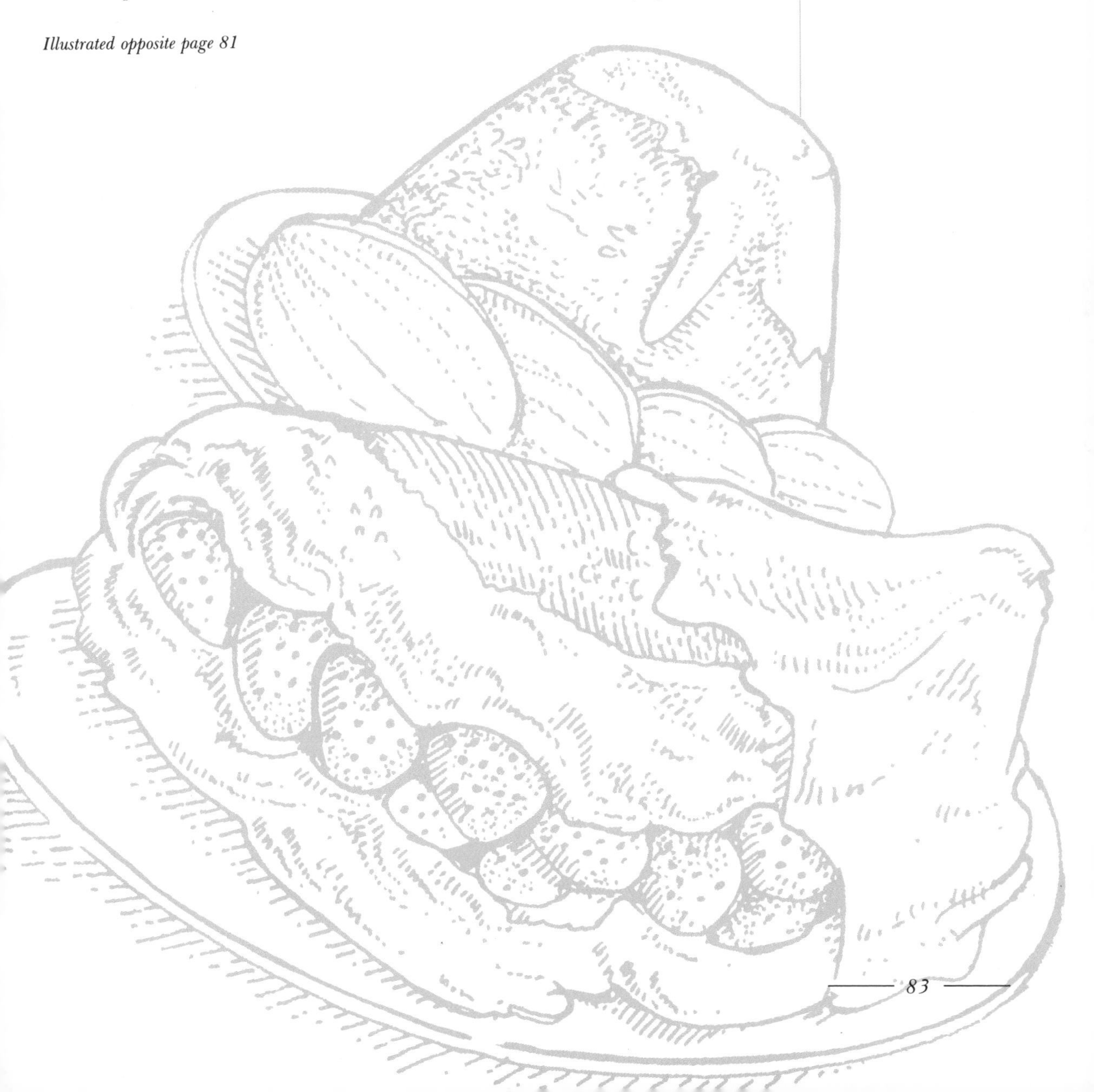

Traditional glazed, heatproof earthenware fondue pot

CHOCOLATE FONDUE

SERVES 4

A sweet fondue is one of the most sociable ways to end a meal, because everyone can relax and linger, selecting a morsel and dipping it into the pot at their leisure. Although there must be quite a few people who have a fondue set hidden away – at one time they were a popular purchase or present – a fondue set is not vital. The sauce can just as easily be kept warm in a heatproof bowl placed over a table-top or plate-warming lamp, or small spirit stove. Fruit for dipping that is to be cut into chunks, such as pineapple, should not be prepared until shortly before the fondue is to be served, and fruits that discolour soon after cutting, such as pears and bananas, should be brushed with lemon juice.

- 225 G/8 OZ PLAIN CHOCOLATE, CHOPPED
- 25 G/1 OZ UNSALTED BUTTER, DICED
- 150 ML/5 FL OZ DOUBLE CREAM
- 2 TBSP DARK RUM

FOR DIPPING:

- FRUIT, SUCH AS PEARS, PINEAPPLE, BANANAS, CHERRIES OR STRAWBERRIES CUT INTO BITE-SIZED PIECES
- FIRM CAKE, SUCH AS MADEIRA, SPONGE OR CHOCOLATE, CUT INTO CHUNKS, FINGER-SHAPED BISCUITS, SUCH AS SPONGE FINGERS
- MARSHMALLOWS

1 Place the chocolate, butter and cream in a heatproof bowl that can also be used for serving and place over a saucepan of hot water. Leave until the chocolate and butter have melted and the mixture is smooth, stirring occasionally. Stir in the rum.

2 Place the bowl or dish over a fondue lamp or table heater and serve with fruit, cake or biscuits for dipping.

FRUMENTY

SERVES 6–8

Frumenty dates from early medieval times. The rich served it as an accompaniment to game and meat; while for the poor, frumenty provided a complete meal. Later it became a dessert, sweetened with honey and dried fruits, which also added texture to this porridge-like dish. A more luxurious pudding, my version contains cream and whisky, and is quite filling, so I advise serving it in small bowls.
Whole-wheat grains are available from good wholefood stores.

- 200 G/7 OZ WHOLE-WHEAT GRAINS
- 400 ML/14 FL OZ MILK
- 85 ML/3 FL OZ DOUBLE CREAM
- 175 G/6 OZ MIXED DRIED FRUITS, SUCH AS PEARS, PEACHES, APRICOTS AND FIGS, CHOPPED
- LONG STRIP OF LEMON RIND
- 3 TBSP WHISKY
- **TO SERVE:**
- HONEY, LEMON JUICE AND CREAM

1 Set the oven to 110°C/225°F/Gas ¼.

2 Put the wheat into a large casserole, pour over warm water to cover generously, then cover the casserole. Place in the oven for about 12 hours.

3 Drain the wheat through a colander, then tip into a saucepan. Stir in the milk, cream, dried fruit and lemon rind and bring slowly to the boil, stirring. Reduce the heat to very low and cook gently, stirring frequently, until nearly all the liquid has been absorbed (about 20–25 minutes).

4 Remove the lemon rind and stir in the whisky. Serve honey, lemon juice and cream separately.

Raspberry Zabaglione

SERVES 4

A potent little pudding. The first time I made it I did not whisk any raspberries with the egg yolk mixture. The result was very pale and its impact seemed greater because it looked so innocuous. It is not only for appearance's sake, though, that the raspberries are whisked in – the zabaglione does taste better that way.

- 4 EGG YOLKS
- 4 TBSP *EAU-DE-VIE DE FRAMBOISE*
- APPROXIMATELY 115 G/4 OZ CASTER SUGAR
- 115 G/4 OZ FRESH RASPBERRIES
- **TO SERVE:**
- CRISP ALMOND BISCUITS

1 Put the egg yolks, eau-de-vie and sugar into a heatproof bowl, then place over a saucepan of hot water. Whisk the mixture until very thick and light; this will take about 10 minutes.

2 Stir in half the raspberries and a little more sugar, if liked, then divide the mixture between 4 glasses or individual serving dishes.

3 Place an equal number of raspberries on top of each zabaglione (they will fall through it) and serve immediately with crisp almond biscuits.

AUSTRIAN PILLOWS WITH PLUM AND RASPBERRY COMPOTE

SERVES 4 – 6

A cousin of Italian savoury gnocchi, Austrian pillows are soft, lightly sweetened balls served with a compote that really brings the pudding to life.

- APPROXIMATELY 1 TBSP VANILLA SUGAR
- JUICE AND FINELY GRATED RIND OF 1 LEMON
- 25 G/1 OZ UNSALTED BUTTER
- 300 G/10 OZ COTTAGE CHEESE, DRAINED AND SIEVED
- 2 EGGS
- 40 G/1½ OZ FINE SEMOLINA

PLUM AND RASPBERRY COMPOTE:

- 350 G/12 OZ RIPE BUT FIRM PLUMS, HALVED AND STONED
- 150 ML/5 FL OZ MEDIUM-BODIED DRY WHITE WINE, SUCH AS VOUVRAY OR OTHER CHENIN BLANC
- 1 BAY LEAF
- APPROXIMATELY 1 TBSP REDCURRANT JELLY
- 225 G/8 OZ RASPBERRIES

1 Put the sugar and lemon juice into a bowl. In a small saucepan, melt 25 g/1 oz butter, then pour into the bowl and beat until frothy. Add the cottage cheese and eggs and beat until smooth. Stir in the semolina, then cover and leave in the refrigerator for 1 hour.

2 To make the compote, put the plums into a saucepan with the wine and bay leaf, then simmer very gently until the plums are just tender. Discard the bay leaf. Stir in the red currant jelly to taste and keep warm over a low heat.

3 Heat a large saucepan of salted water to simmering point. Using 2 wetted dessertspoons, form the mixture into small dumplings and lower into the water. Poach for about 10 minutes, or until they rise to the surface. Using a slotted spoon, transfer the dumplings to absorbent kitchen paper to drain briefly.

4 Remove the compote from the heat and stir in the raspberries. Serve warm with the pillows.

Illustrated opposite page 81

Slicing mangoes:

Remove the mango skin using a potato peeler

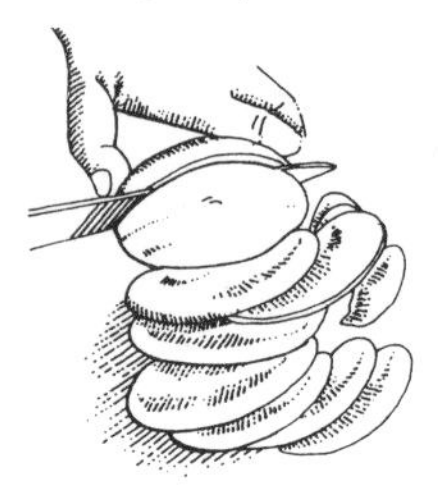

Slice through the flesh to the stone in the centre

Making coconut milk:

Squeeze the cloth hard over the bowl to extract as much liquid as possible

MANGOES WITH STICKY RICE

SERVES 4

Thai food has been rapidly gaining in popularity, and Mangoes with Sticky Rice is the most popular Thai pudding, which will come as no surprise to anyone who has eaten it. Ripe mangoes are the most marvellous of fruits, with a haunting, exotic fragrance, texture and taste, and Thailand grows some of the best. Sticky rice is available from Thai and other Oriental food stores.

- 225 G/8 OZ STICKY RICE OR PUDDING RICE, SOAKED OVERNIGHT IN COLD WATER
- 225 ML/8 FL OZ COCONUT MILK (SEE NOTE)
- PINCH OF SALT
- 2–4 TBSP SUGAR, TO TASTE
- 2 LARGE RIPE MANGOES, PEELED AND HALVED
- 3 TBSP COCONUT CREAM (SEE NOTE)

1 Line a steaming basket with a double thickness of muslin. Half fill a saucepan with water and bring to the boil.

2 Drain and rinse the rice thoroughly and put it into the steaming basket. Cover the basket, place over the saucepan and steam over simmering water for 30 minutes.

3 Just before the rice is ready, in a large bowl, stir together the coconut milk, salt and sugar to taste until the sugar has dissolved. Stir in the warm rice, cover and leave for 30 minutes.

4 Thinly slice the mangoes by cutting lengthways through the flesh to the stone. Discard the stones. Spoon the rice into a mound in the centre of 4 warm serving plates and arrange the mango slices around, and decorate with fresh mint sprigs, if liked. Pour a little coconut cream over the rice and serve immediately.

NOTE: Coconut milk is not the liquid inside a coconut, but made from shredded coconut flesh that has been soaked in water. To make it, and the coconut cream for this recipe, pour 300 ml/10 fl oz boiling milk that has not been homogenized over 225 g/8 oz desiccated coconut. Leave until cooled, then pour into a blender or food processor, mix for 1 minute, then leave for 30 minutes. Tip into a sieve lined with muslin or fine cloth and squeeze the cloth hard to extract as much liquid as possible. Leave the liquid to stand and the cream will rise to the top.

Illustrated opposite page 81

PLUM OR STRAWBERRY KNÖDELN

SERVES 3–6

I have used part of the original Austrian name for this dish because the English translation is dumplings, but the unfortunate associations with solid suet pastry that this title has in Britain do a great disservice to the delicate covering of this recipe. The plums can have their stones replaced by marzipan, walnuts or almonds. Traditionally, the dumplings are rolled in breadcrumbs that have been fried in plenty of butter until crisp and golden then dusted with icing sugar. Crushed sweet biscuits can be used instead of breadcrumbs and the final icing sugar dusting omitted. I like crushed macaroons or amaretti biscuits, and finely grated plain chocolate or cocoa powder are very good with strawberries.

- 40 G/1½ OZ UNSALTED BUTTER
- 1 WHOLE EGG, SIZE 2, BEATEN
- 1 EGG YOLK, SIZE 3
- 350 G/12 OZ CREAM CHEESE, SIEVED
- 1½ TBSP SOURED CREAM
- APPROXIMATELY 1½ TSP VANILLA CASTER SUGAR, TO TASTE
- FEW DROPS ALMOND ESSENCE
- 40 G/1½ OZ PLAIN FLOUR
- 20 G/¾ OZ CORNFLOUR
- 12 SMALLISH RIPE PLUMS OR 12 STRAWBERRIES
- 135–175 G/4½–6 OZ MARZIPAN OR 12 WALNUT HALVES OR ALMONDS (OPTIONAL)
- **TO SERVE:**
- SABAYON SAUCE (SEE PAGE 185) OR COLD CUSTARD (SEE PAGE 181)

1 Beat the butter until fluffy, then gradually beat in the egg and egg yolk, then mix in the cream cheese, soured cream, sugar and almond essence. Sieve together the flour and cornflour, then, using a slotted spoon, stir into the cheese mixture and mix well until smooth. Cover and chill in the refrigerator for 30 minutes.

2 If using plums, carefully remove the stones and fill the cavities with a piece of marzipan, a walnut half or an almond, if liked.

3 On a lightly floured surface, gently roll out the dough to about 5 mm–1.25 cm/¼–½ inch thick, then cut into 12 approximately 12.5 cm/5 inch squares. Place a plum or strawberry in the centre of each. Brush the edges with a little water and fold the dough over the fruit to form a package, pressing the edges to seal.

4 Bring a wide saucepan of water to the boil, carefully lower in some of the dumplings so they are not crowded and poach for 12–15 minutes.

5 Using a slotted spoon, transfer the dumplings to a plate lined with a cloth and keep warm while cooking the remaining dumplings. Serve warm with Sabayon Sauce or cold Custard.

PASTRIES

CHAPTER FOUR

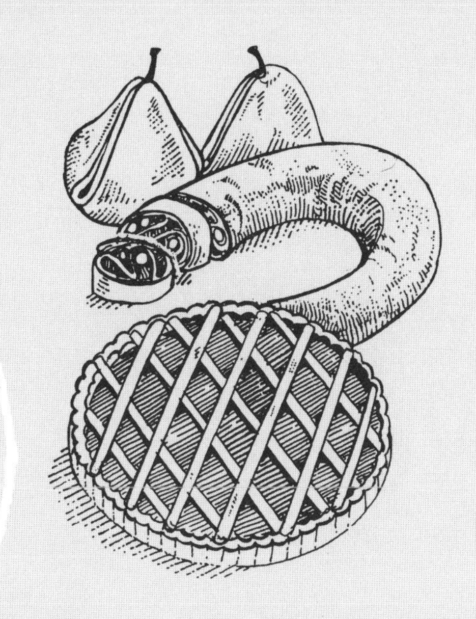

The Greeks made a very simple form of pastry from flour, honey and sesame seeds about twenty-four centuries ago. Although a very similar type of pastry is still made in the Middle East, pastry has seen many changes since then. Fat, preferably butter, is added to make it richer and more tender, eggs may also be included and the flour will be from appropriate strains of wheat. And whereas at one time the pastry was just a container for a filling, today it is just as, sometimes even more, important than the filling, for it adds taste and texture, and provides a vehicle for adding other flavours such as spices, to complement and enhance the filling. Success with pastry seems to be a question of attitude. The people who do not have any trouble seem to be those who do not expect any problems, whereas those who approach it timidly, and perhaps try too hard, seem to be the ones who experience failure. So approach it with confidence. Be aware before you start what you should be doing and understand what happens if you do not; take a little care, and feather-light, melting, crisp pastry for pies, tarts, flans, tartlets and turnovers will be yours.

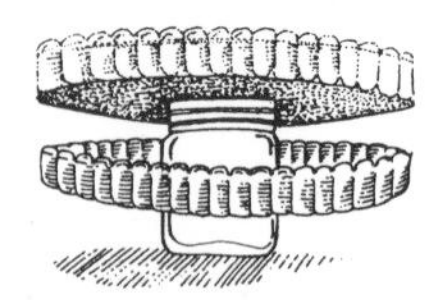

Leave the flan or tart to cool slightly, then place it centrally on a jar. Gently ease down the outer ring

SHORTCRUST, PÂTE SUCRÉE AND PUFF PASTRY

☞ Recipes for pastry can vary according to the filling ingredients.
☞ Sugar in *pâte sucrée* not only makes it sweeter, but also more crisp, more difficult to handle and more likely to scorch when baked.
☞ Egg yolks add richness and enable you to patch the dough more easily, if necessary, after rolling out.
☞ Make sure the ingredients, equipment and your hands are cool before starting to make the pastry and throughout the process. If the dough becomes sticky because it is too warm, cover it and put it in the refrigerator to cool and firm up. Equipment can also be popped in the refrigerator. To cool your hands, allow cold running water to flow over them and your wrists; dry well before handling the pastry.
☞ A cool atmosphere is also important, so avoid making pastry when your kitchen is hot. In hot weather, if your kitchen becomes hot during the day, try to make the pastry in the morning before it heats up or in the evening after it has cooled down. If central heating makes it hot, try turning it off in the kitchen for a short while before making the pastry and during the process.
☞ Handle the dough quickly, lightly and sensitively, as heavy or over-handling will make the dough sticky and tough, and will prevent puff pastry rising.
☞ Cover the dough and leave it in the refrigerator for at least 20–30 minutes before it is rolled out for the final shaping and refrigerate it again afterwards for at least the same amount of time, before baking it. Puff pastry must also be chilled in between the rollings and foldings.
☞ If the dough is left so long in the refrigerator that it becomes hard, allow it to soften a little at room temperature before rolling it out.
☞ When rolling out, sprinkle a light covering of flour over the work surface and rolling pin and form the dough to the shape required, i.e. round or rectangular. Roll away from you in short, quick movements in one direction only, run a metal palette knife under the dough and then turn it.
☞ Even if the dough becomes sticky, do not sprinkle flour directly onto it, as this can produce tough pastry.
☞ When making pastry cases, always use metal, not heatproof glass, earthenware or ceramic containers.
☞ To prevent pastry from becoming soggy when filled with a cooked or liquid filling, such as a custard mixture, bake it blind first (see opposite). Once a filling has been added, the pastry must be baked immediately. Further insurance against soggy pastry is given by brushing the baked pastry with egg white and never adding a hot filling to pastry, whether raw or baked.
☞ *Pâte sucrée* and nut pastries are fragile when they are taken from the oven, so leave them to stand for a few minutes before moving them.
☞ Pastries are at their best if eaten fresh from the oven, either whilst still warm or within a few hours.

TO LINE A FLAN TIN OR RING WITH PASTRY

Butter the flan tin or a flan ring placed on a buttered baking sheet. On a lightly floured surface, using a lightly floured rolling pin, roll the dough out thinly to about 4.25–6.25 cm/1½–2½ inches larger than the diameter of the ring, depending on the depth of the sides of the tin or ring. Lightly brush away any surplus flour from the surface of the dough. Carefully roll the dough back over the rolling pin and lift it over the centre of the ring. Unroll the dough from the rolling pin and allow it to loosely fall to the shape of the ring. Working from the centre, carefully ease the dough into shape, gently but firmly pressing it into the angle between the base and the sides so that it fits snugly. If using a fluted flan ring, pay particular attention to easing the dough into the curves, especially at the base. Leave the dough to relax for 20 minutes or so, then remove the excess dough by passing the rolling pin quickly and firmly across the top of the flan ring. Lightly prick the base with the prongs of a fork, cover and chill.

The thickness of the pastry will vary according not only to the type of pastry, but also to the particular use to which it is being put – different tarts are more enjoyable with different thicknesses of pastry.

Lining tartlet tins:

Lay the pastry over the tins

TO LINE TARTLET OR BARQUETTE TINS WITH PASTRY

Group the tins together on a baking tray. Roll the pastry out thinly, fold it back over the rolling pin, lift it over the tins, then reroll it onto them. With a small ball of floured dough, ease the pastry into the shape of the tins. Roll the rolling pin firmly over the top of the tins to remove excess pastry.

Use a small ball of dough to ease in the pastry

TO BAKE PASTRY BLIND

Lay a piece of greaseproof paper on the base of the pastry case and cover with just enough dried beans or ceramic baking beans to weigh the pastry down. Bake in a preheated oven for about 10 minutes if it is to be baked further after filling or until the pastry is set and very lightly coloured. Remove the baking beans and greaseproof paper. If the pastry in the base of the case appears to be too pale, return it to the oven for a few minutes to colour a little more. If the pastry is not to be baked again after filling, return it to the oven for about 10–15 minutes after removing the lining paper until the pastry is light golden brown and completely set.

To bake pastry blind:

Cover the greaseproof paper with an even layer of baking beans

Choux pastry:

Beat until the mixture comes cleanly away from the sides of the pan

Prick a small hole in the base of baked choux pastries to allow steam to escape

RIGHT (from top to bottom): Black Forest Puffs (see page 119); Gâteau Pithiviers (see page 120); King-Size Fig Newton (see page 117).

FREEZING

☞ UNCOOKED, UNSHAPED DOUGH:
Open freeze, then wrap in heavy-duty polythene and freeze for up to 4 months. To use, thaw in the refrigerator overnight, or at a cool room temperature for about 2 hours before using.

☞ UNCOOKED, SHAPED DOUGH:
Roll the dough into shapes for pie lids, or use to line flan tins or rings, or tartlet cases. Open freeze, then remove from the container and wrap in heavy-duty polythene. Interleave pie lids with greaseproof paper and overwrap in heavy-duty polythene. Freeze for up to 4 months. To use, return pastry cases to the containers. Bake from frozen, giving them an extra 5 minutes or so in the oven. The same applies to pie lids.

☞ COOKED PASTRY:
Cool quickly, open freeze, then wrap in heavy-duty polythene and freeze for up to 3 months. To use, refresh in an oven preheated to 200°C/400°F/Gas 6 for about 10 minutes, depending on the filling.

CHOUX PASTRY

☞ Have the flour weighed out by the hob so that it can be added immediately the liquid comes to the boil.

☞ Dice the butter so that it melts quickly.

☞ Once the butter has melted, bring the liquid quickly to the boil, then immediately remove the pan from the heat and add all the flour in one go. If the flour is added in stages it will cook into lumps.

☞ Return the pan to a low heat and cook the flour, beating with a wooden spoon or, better still, a hand-held mixer, for about ½–1 minute until it comes cleanly away from the sides and base of the pan.

☞ Allow the dough to cool slightly before adding the eggs, otherwise they will begin to cook and so be incapable of entrapping air.

☞ Beat in the eggs gradually and beat well after each addition to enable as much air as possible to be incorporated. If the eggs are added too quickly, the dough will be too soft and you will then not be able to shape it properly and it will not rise.

☞ The outside of choux pastry shapes, especially large ones, often appears cooked, while some of the dough inside is still moist, so pierce a small hole in the side of the shape to allow the steam to escape and return it to the oven with the heat turned off for a few minutes to dry out.

☞ For the best results, choux pastry really should be cooked soon after it has been made, but it can be kept for up to about 4 hours, although it will not rise so well. To prevent a skin forming on the dough, stretch a piece of cling film across the top of the saucepan.
☞ Choux pastries are at their best on the day they are made, but they can be kept in an airtight container or a plastic bag for 1 or at the most 2 days. Pop briefly in a fairly hot oven to refresh them, then allow to cool before using.
☞ Choux pastries quite quickly become soggy after being filled, so should be eaten within an hour or so.

FREEZING

Baked, unfilled choux pastry can be frozen for up to 3 months. Open freeze, then, as the pastry is fragile, pack carefully into a rigid, freezer-proof container. To use, crisp the pastry up, from frozen, on a baking sheet in an oven preheated to 200°C/400°F/ Gas 6 for 5–7 minutes.

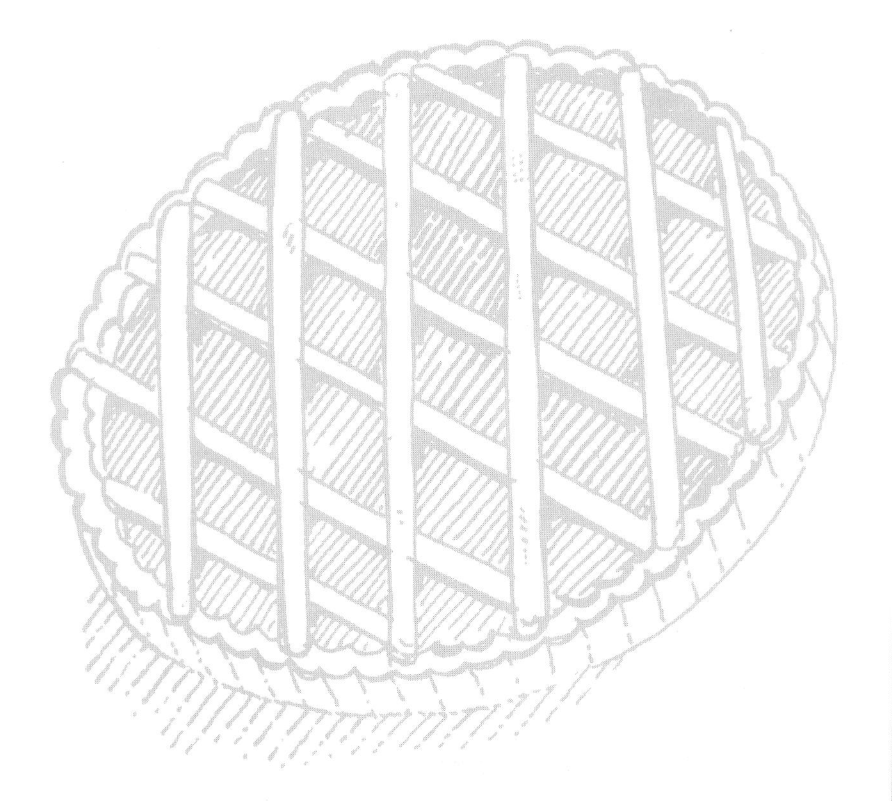

LEFT (from top to bottom): Walnut Tartlets (see page 128); Candied Peel Tart (see page 102); Really Good Lemon Meringue Pie (see page 106).

*B*ASIC SHORTCRUST PASTRY

MAKES APPROXIMATELY 375 G/13 OZ

...

- 225 G/8 OZ PLAIN FLOUR
- 115 G/4 OZ UNSALTED BUTTER, DICED
- COLD WATER

1 Sift the flour into a bowl, toss in the butter, then, using your fingertips, rub into the flour until the mixture resembles breadcrumbs.

2 Sprinkle about 2 tablespoons cold water over the surface of the flour mixture, then lightly mix it in using a round-bladed knife until the mixture forms large lumps; add a little more water if necessary.

3 Using your fingertips again, lightly form the lumps into a smooth ball that will leave the bowl clean, transfer to a lightly floured surface and knead lightly until smooth and free from cracks. Form into a ball, wrap in cling film and place in the refrigerator for at least 30 minutes before rolling out.

Basic Pâte Sucrée

MAKES APPROXIMATELY 250–300 G/9–10 OZ

...

- 125 G/4½ OZ PLAIN FLOUR
- SMALL PINCH OF SALT
- 70 G/2½ OZ UNSALTED BUTTER, AT ROOM TEMPERATURE
- 2 EGG YOLKS, BEATEN
- 15–40 G/½–1½ OZ CASTER SUGAR

1 Sift the flour and salt onto a cold work surface and form a well in the centre. Pound the butter with a rolling pin to soften it slightly, then chop it roughly with a cold knife. Put the lumps of butter into the well with the egg and sugar, then quickly and lightly blend them together by 'pecking' at them with the fingertips until they are just beginning to come together and look rather like rough scrambled egg.

2 Sprinkle a little of the flour over the butter/egg mixture, then, as lightly and quickly as possible, draw all the ingredients together by chopping through them with a cold round-bladed knife whilst at the same time drawing free flour from the edges of the pile into the centre with a smooth, flowing action.

3 When there is no free fat or flour to be seen and the mixture resembles breadcrumbs, draw it lightly into a ball with your fingertips, then knead gently by pushing the dough away from you with the heel of one hand, then gathering up the dough with a pastry scraper or palette knife and repeating for a minute or so until the dough peels easily from the work surface. Form into a ball, wrap in cling film and place in the refrigerator for at least 30 minutes before rolling out.

Making pâte sucrée:

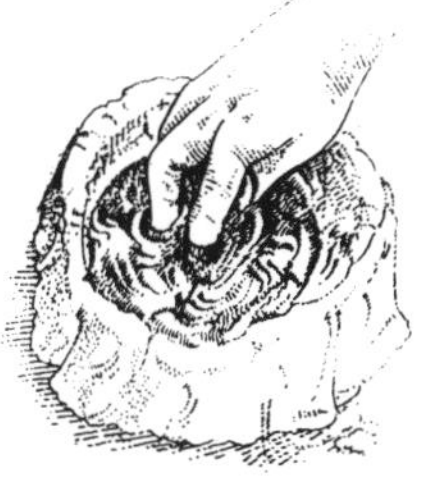

With the fingertips, mix together the butter, egg yolk, sugar and water

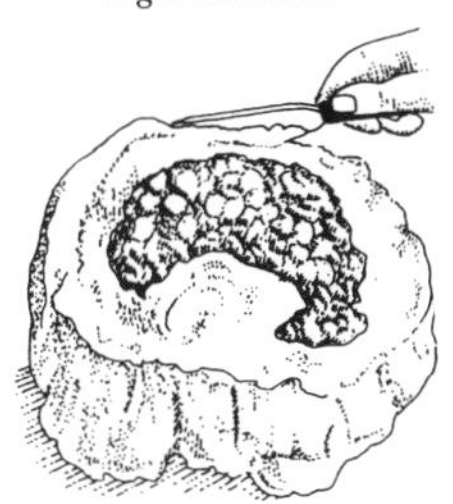

Gradually draw in the flour, using a palette knife

Chop in the flour until the mixture resembles crumbs

Knead the dough with the heel of the hand

Nut Pastry

MAKES APPROXIMATELY 300 G/10 OZ

...

- 125 G/4½ OZ PLAIN FLOUR
- SMALL PINCH OF SALT
- 65 G/2¼ OZ UNSALTED BUTTER, AT ROOM TEMPERATURE
- 1 EGG YOLK, BEATEN
- 40 G/1½ OZ NUTS, GROUND
- 40 G/1½ OZ CASTER SUGAR (OPTIONAL)

Make in exactly the same way as Pâte Sucrée, adding the nuts with the egg yolk.

BASIC PUFF PASTRY

MAKES 450 G / 1 LB

...

- 225 G/8 OZ PLAIN FLOUR
- PINCH OF SALT
- 1 TSP LEMON JUICE
- COLD WATER
- 225 G/8 OZ UNSALTED BUTTER, AT ROOM TEMPERATURE

1 Sift together the flour and salt, then add the lemon juice and sufficient water to form into a soft, pliable but not sticky dough. Knead it into a smooth ball, cover and place in the refrigerator for 30 minutes.

2 Place the butter between two sheets of greaseproof paper or cling film and beat it with a rolling pin until it is soft and malleable and about 1.25 cm/½ inch thick.

3 On a lightly floured surface, using a lightly floured rolling pin, roll the dough out to a square about 7.5 mm/¼ inch thick around the edges with a slightly thicker pad of dough in the centre. Place the butter on this pad and fold the corners of the dough around it, overlapping the edges very slightly, so they meet in the centre. Gently press the block of dough with the rolling pin at 1.25 cm/½ inch intervals across its surface until it has grown slightly, then roll it out to a large rectangle. Fold the two ends of the rectangle so they meet in the centre, then fold the whole piece in half so that it resembles a book. Rotate this to the normal reading position of a book with the folded side as the spine. Cover and place in the refrigerator for 30 minutes.

4 Repeat the rolling and folding five times, chilling the dough after each one for a minimum of 20–30 minutes. Then roll the dough once more before covering and chill for at least 2 hours before giving the final shaping.

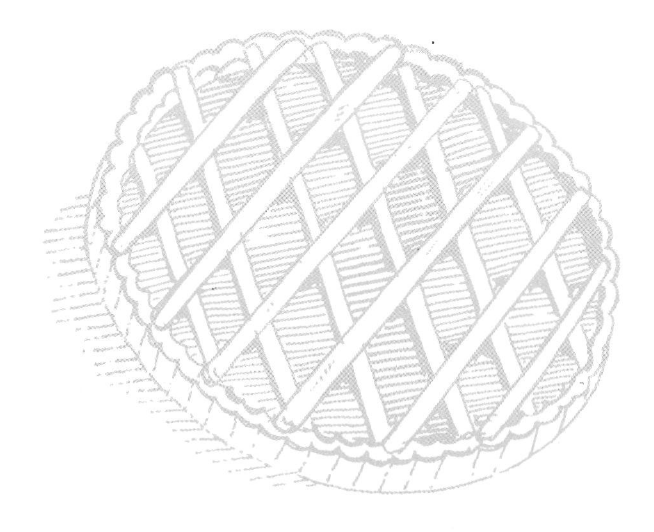

RHUBARB, SOURED CREAM AND GINGER FLAN

SERVES 4–6

Rhubarb, held in crisp, ginger-spiked pastry and surrounded by a creamy filling flavoured with ginger syrup, tastes heavenly.

- 175 G/6 OZ PLAIN FLOUR
- 40 G/1 ½ OZ ICING SUGAR
- 1 ½ TSP GROUND GINGER
- 40 G/1 ½ OZ UNSALTED BUTTER
- 55 G/2 OZ FULL-FAT SOFT CHEESE
- COLD WATER
- 1 EGG WHITE, BEATEN
- **FILLING:**
- 700 G/1 ½ LB RHUBARB, CUT INTO 2.5 CM/1 IN LENGTHS
- 85 G/3 OZ LIGHT MUSCOVADO SUGAR
- 1 TBSP WATER
- 150 ML/5 FL OZ SOURED CREAM
- 4 EGG YOLKS, BEATEN
- 2–3 TBSP SYRUP FROM A JAR OF PRESERVED STEM GINGER
- **DECORATION:**
- THIN STRIPS OF PRESERVED STEM GINGER (OPTIONAL)

Prick the base of the pastry case with a fork, to prevent the pastry rising during baking

1 Sift the flour, icing sugar and ground ginger into a bowl. Cut in the butter and cheese, then lightly rub in using your fingertips until the mixture resembles breadcrumbs. Stir in sufficient very cold water to make a firm dough. Cover and place in the refrigerator for 30 minutes.

2 Butter a 22.5 cm/9 inch flan tin. On a lightly floured surface, roll out the pastry and use to line the flan tin. Prick the base of the pastry case, then cover and place in the refrigerator for another 30 minutes.

3 Meanwhile, make the filling. Gently cook the rhubarb with 1 tablespoon of the sugar and the water in a wide saucepan until slightly softened but still holding its shape. Drain and leave to cool. Boil the cooking juices until well reduced and syrupy. Cool.

4 Set the oven to 200°C/400°F/Gas 6 and put a baking sheet in the oven.

5 Place the flan tin on the baking sheet and bake the pastry case blind for 10 minutes (see page 95). Remove the paper and beans, brush the base and sides of the pastry case with egg white and return to the oven for a few minutes. Leave to cool.

6 Lower the oven temperature to 150°C/300°F/Gas 2.

7 Using a slotted spoon, transfer the rhubarb to the pastry case. Stir together the rhubarb juices, soured cream, the remaining sugar, the egg yolks and the ginger syrup. Carefully pour over the rhubarb and place in the oven for 25–30 minutes until just set in the centre. Serve warm or at room temperature with thin strips of stem ginger sprinkled over, if liked.

CANDIED PEEL TART

SERVES 4 – 6

This is one of my mother's favourites. It is very good made from mixed candied peel that comes in a tub, but it is even better if it is made from separate, large pieces of candied orange, citron and lemon peel; remove excess sugar from the pieces before chopping and mix in roughly equal quantities.

- *PÂTE SUCRÉE* MADE WITH 175 G/6 OZ PLAIN FLOUR, 85 G/3 OZ UNSALTED BUTTER, 2 EGG YOLKS, 3 TBSP ICING SUGAR (SEE PAGE 99)
- 1 EGG WHITE
- **FILLING:**
- 2 EGGS, SIZE 2
- 2 EGG YOLKS, SIZE 2
- 150 G/5 OZ CASTER SUGAR
- 175 G/6 OZ UNSALTED BUTTER, MELTED AND COOLED
- 115 G/4 OZ CANDIED PEEL, QUITE FINELY CHOPPED
- 2 TBSP COINTREAU (OPTIONAL)
- **DECORATION:**
- ICING SUGAR, FOR DUSTING (OPTIONAL)
- TOASTED FLAKED ALMONDS (OPTIONAL)

1 Butter a 22.5 cm/9 inch flan tin. On a lightly floured surface, roll out the pastry and use to line the tin. Prick the base of the pastry case, cover and place in the refrigerator for 30 minutes.

2 Set the oven to 200°C/400°F/Gas 6. Place a baking sheet in the oven.

3 Place the flan tin on the baking sheet and bake the pastry case blind for 10 minutes (see page 95). Remove the paper and beans, brush the base and sides of the pastry with egg white and return to the oven for a couple of minutes. Leave to cool.

4 Lower the oven temperature to 180°C/350°F/Gas 4.

5 Mix together the eggs, egg yolks, sugar, butter, mixed peel and Cointreau, if using, then pour into the pastry case. Bake for about 30 minutes until very lightly set in the centre and crisp and lightly browned on top. Serve warm, dusted with icing sugar and toasted flaked almonds sprinkled on top, if liked.

Illustrated opposite page 97

GREENGAGE AND ALMOND SHUTTLES

SERVES 4

These pastries are called shuttles because their shape resembles the shuttles used with old-fashioned weaving looms. As it would not be worth making puff pastry specifically for this recipe, I have given the prepared weight so that you could either cut the required weight from pastry you have already made or from a piece of commercial puff pastry. When greengages are not available, substitute ripe plums.

- 55 G/2 OZ UNSALTED BUTTER, DICED
- 55 G/2 OZ CASTER SUGAR
- 1 EGG, SIZE 3, BEATEN
- 55 G/2 OZ ALMONDS, GROUND
- FEW DROPS OF ORANGE FLOWER WATER OR PINCH OF CRUSHED CARDAMOM SEEDS (OPTIONAL)
- APPROXIMATELY 225 G/8 OZ PREPARED WEIGHT PUFF PASTRY (SEE PAGE 100)
- 6 RIPE GREENGAGES, HALVED AND STONED
- 1 EGG, BEATEN, FOR GLAZING

1 Beat the butter with the sugar until light and pale. Gradually stir in the egg, then stir in the ground almonds. Flavour with orange flower water, or crushed cardamom seeds, if liked.

2 On a lightly floured surface, roll out the pastry to approximately 50 cm/20 inches square. Using a large sharp knife, trim the edges, then cut the pastry into 4 squares. Divide the almond mixture between the squares, placing it to one side of the centre and leaving a border around the edge. Nestle 3 greengage halves closely together in a single layer on the almond mixture. Brush the edges of the pastry with water, then fold the uncovered dough over the greengages and press the edges firmly together to seal. With the point of a small sharp knife, cut 3 short slashes in the top of each pastry. Place the pastries on a baking tray, cover and chill in the refrigerator for 30 minutes.

3 Set the oven to 200°C/400°F/Gas 6. Brush the pastries with beaten egg and bake for about 25 minutes until the pastry is crisp and golden. Cool slightly before serving.

Illustrated opposite page 17

Black Cherry Strudel

SERVES 6–8

I really enjoy making phyllo (filo) pastry. Because it takes a little while and has to be done gently and at a quite leisurely pace, I find it very relaxing. You will find it easier to stretch the dough if you work it on a table that you can walk around.

- 225 G/8 OZ PLAIN FLOUR
- 1 EGG, BEATEN
- 175 ML/6 FL OZ LUKEWARM WATER
- ½ TSP LEMON JUICE
- 115 G/4 OZ UNSALTED BUTTER, MELTED
- **FILLING:**
- 350 G/12 OZ RICOTTA OR CURD CHEESE, SIEVED
- 100 G/3½ OZ DEMERARA SUGAR
- 5–6 TBSP SINGLE CREAM
- 1 EGG, BEATEN
- FINELY GRATED RIND OF 1 LEMON
- 225 G/8 OZ RIPE BLACK CHERRIES, OR 1 × 350 G/12 OZ CAN BLACK CHERRIES IN NATURAL JUICE, WELL DRAINED
- ICING SUGAR, FOR DUSTING
- **TO SERVE:**
- VANILLA DAIRY ICE CREAM OR SINGLE CREAM

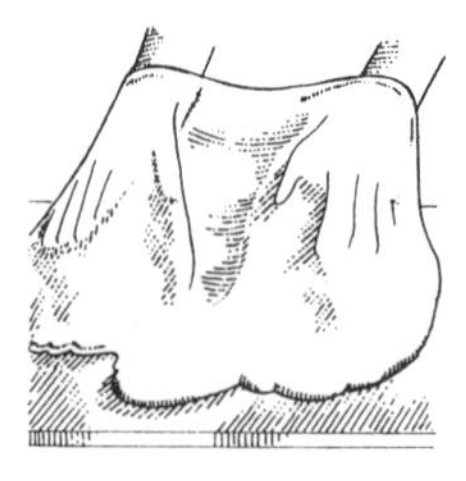

Gradually stretch the dough over the backs of your hands

1 Sift the flour onto a work surface and form a well in the centre. Mix together the egg, water and lemon juice, then pour into the well in the flour. Using your finger tips, quickly draw the dry ingredients into the liquids to form coarse crumbs. Add a little extra water if the crumbs seem dry. Form into a fairly soft ball. Flour the work surface and knead the dough by forming it into a short sausage, picking it up by alternate ends and bringing it firmly down onto the surface, for 5–7 minutes until smooth and shiny. Cover with an upturned bowl and leave for 30 minutes.

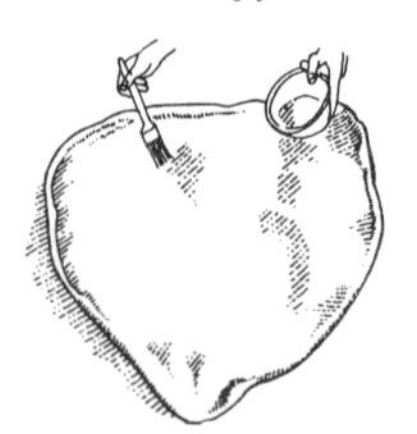

Brush the dough with melted butter

2 Set the oven to 190°C/375°F/Gas 5. Butter a large baking sheet.

3 To make the filling, in a bowl, beat the cheese and sugar, then gradually beat in the cream, egg and lemon rind.

Roll up the filled dough with the help of the sheet

4 Cover the table with a clean sheet or other large piece of similar material, sprinkle it lightly with flour then roll out the dough, using a lightly floured rolling pin, to as large a square as you can make it. Cover with a damp towel and leave for 15 minutes.

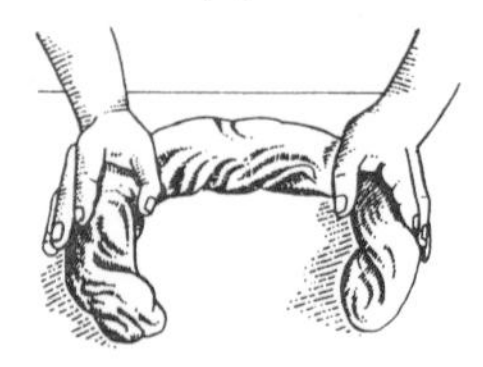

Form into a horse-shoe shape with the seam underneath

5 Sprinkle flour over the backs of your hands and place them under the centre of the dough. Slowly work outwards, gradually stretching the dough evenly with both hands; do not worry if small holes appear. Repeat across the surface of the dough until it is about 1 metre/1 yard square. If the edge is very thick, cut it off. Brush the dough with melted butter, spread the cream cheese mixture over, leaving a narrow border around the edge, then cover with the cherries. Trim the edges of the dough. Roll it up with the aid of the sheet. Transfer the roll to the baking sheet, with the seam underneath, and shape it into a horseshoe. Brush with melted butter and bake for 30–40 minutes until light brown and crisp. Carefully transfer to a wire rack and dust with icing sugar. Serve sliced with vanilla dairy ice cream or single cream.

OLD ENGLISH APPLE PIE

SERVES 6

Pies of apples mixed with oranges plus dried fruits for natural sweetness were popular in Georgian times. Adjust the amounts of dried fruits, candied peel and spices if they are not to your taste.

- SHORTCRUST PASTRY MADE WITH 225 G/8 OZ PLAIN FLOUR, 115 G/4 OZ UNSALTED BUTTER AND 2–3 TBSP COLD WATER (SEE PAGE 98)
- 55 G/2 OZ PLUMP SULTANAS
- 25 G/1 OZ CURRANTS
- 55 G/2 OZ PLUMP RAISINS
- 55 G/2 OZ CANDIED PEEL, CHOPPED
- 3 TBSP RUM, BRANDY, WHISKY OR SHERRY
- 1 EGG WHITE, BEATEN
- 550 G/1¼ LB COX'S ORANGE PIPPIN OR REINETTE APPLES
- 2 ORANGES, PEELED AND SLICED
- 1 JUICY LEMON, PEELED AND SLICED, OR FINELY GRATED RIND AND JUICE OF 1 LEMON
- 55 G/2 OZ DARK MUSCOVADO SUGAR
- ½–¾ TSP FRESHLY GRATED NUTMEG
- 1–2 TSP GROUND CINNAMON
- 40 G/1½ OZ FLAKED ALMONDS
- 25 G/1 OZ UNSALTED BUTTER
- 1 EGG YOLK BEATEN WITH 1 TBSP WATER
- CASTER SUGAR, FOR DREDGING

1 Butter a 22.5 cm/9 inch pie dish. On a lightly floured surface, roll out two-thirds of the pastry and use it to line the dish. Prick the base of the pastry case, cover and place in the refrigerator for 30 minutes, along with the remaining pastry, which should be wrapped in cling film or greaseproof paper.

2 Stir the sultanas, currants, raisins, candied peel and rum, brandy, whisky or sherry together in a bowl.

3 Set the oven to 190°C/375°F/Gas 5 and place a baking sheet in the oven.

4 Place the pie dish on the baking sheet and bake blind for 10 minutes (see page 95) until set and lightly coloured. Remove the paper and beans, brush the base and sides of the pastry case with beaten egg white and return to the oven for 5 minutes.

5 Roll out the remaining pastry to make a lid for the pie dish. Peel, core and thickly slice the apples, then place in the pastry case with the orange and lemon slices, or lemon rind and juice, dried fruits and their soaking liquor, the sugar and spices. Quickly fry the almonds in the butter until golden then scatter evenly over the filling and pour over the butter. Brush the edges of the pastry case with water, then cover the pie with the pastry lid, pressing the edges well together to seal. With the point of a sharp knife, cut two slashes in the top. Use the pastry trimmings to decorate the top of the pie. Brush with beaten egg yolk, dredge with caster sugar, then bake for 35–40 minutes until the pastry is golden brown and the fruit tender. Serve warm.

Illustrated opposite page 112

Really Good Lemon Meringue Pie

SERVES 6

There are some things that one hankers for from childhood days. For me, the type of lemon meringue pie that was popular when I was a child is not one of them, as the filling, made from packet ingredients, had a distinctive, rather gluey texture. Needless to say, this pie is nothing like that. The filling resembles a clean, fresh-tasting, light home-made lemon curd, which is highlighted by the hint of cardamom in the pastry, and the cloud of meringue on top has a delicious, light lemony flavour.

- *Pâte Sucrée* made with 150 g/5 oz plain flour; 100 g/3½ oz unsalted butter, diced; approximately ¾–1 tsp cardamom seeds, dry-fried then ground; 2 tsp icing sugar and 2 tbps white wine or water (see page 99)

- **Filling and meringue:**
- finely grated rind and juice of 2 large, juicy lemons
- 250 g/9 oz caster sugar
- 2 whole eggs
- 3 eggs, separated
- 100 g/3½ oz unsalted butter, diced
- finely grated rind of 1 more large lemon

1 First, make the pastry. Sift the flour into a bowl, toss in the butter, then rub in until the mixture resembles breadcrumbs. Stir in the cardamom seeds, icing sugar and sufficient wine or water to make a soft but not sticky dough. Cover and place in the refrigerator for 30 minutes.

2 Butter a deep 20 cm/8 inch flan tin. On a lightly floured surface, roll out the pastry and use to line the tin. Prick the base of the pastry case, cover and chill for 30 minutes.

3 Set the oven to 190°C/375°F/Gas 5. Place a baking sheet in the oven.

4 Place the flan tin on the baking sheet and bake the pastry case blind for 10 minutes (see page 95). Remove the paper and beans and return the pastry case to the oven for 5–10 minutes until pale biscuit coloured. Leave to cool.

5 To make the filling, put the lemon rind and juice, 115 g/4 oz of the sugar and the whole eggs and egg yolks in a heatproof bowl. Place over a saucepan of hot water and gradually stir in the butter using a wooden spoon. Continue to stir for about 15–20 minutes until the mixture thickens. Leave to cool.

6 To make the meringue, in a clean, dry bowl, whisk the 3 egg whites until soft peaks form, then gradually whisk in the remaining sugar, whisking well after each addition, until the mixture is stiff and shiny. Add the rind of the extra lemon with the last addition.

7 Spoon the lemon mixture evenly into the pastry case and cover completely with the meringue, taking particular care that there are no gaps next to the pastry shell. Bake for 10–15 minutes until the meringue is lightly browned and crisp on top but still soft inside.

VARIATION:
To make a meringue nest topping, reserve 1½ tablespoons of the lemon mixture. Using a palette knife, spread two-thirds of the meringue over the lemon mixture in the pastry case to make a plateau about 1.25 cm/½ inch high. Put the remaining meringue into a piping bag fitted with a 1.25 cm/½ inch plain nozzle and pipe 8 small nests on top. Bake for 10–15 minutes. Before serving, divide the reserved lemon mixture between the nests.

Illustrated opposite page 97

Baklava

MAKES 20–25 PIECES

Baklava does not have to be the sickly-sweet 'lump' that it all too often is. Use a good quality honey, plenty of moist, fresh nuts, include some wine in the syrup and add some spices and lime rind and juice to relieve the sweetness and you have a luscious pastry. An unconventional addition that I use occasionally is a layer of sliced fresh figs or nectarines placed on the last layer of filling.

- 225 G/8 OZ UNSALTED BUTTER, MELTED
- 1 × 450 G/1 LB PACKET PHYLLO (FILO) PASTRY (ABOUT 20 SHEETS)
- **FILLING:**
- 225 G/8 OZ PISTACHIO NUTS, FINELY CHOPPED
- 225 G/8 OZ BLANCHED ALMONDS, FINELY CHOPPED
- 50 G/1¾ OZ LIGHT MUSCOVADO SUGAR
- 1 TSP GROUND CINNAMON
- PINCH OF GROUND CLOVES
- **SYRUP:**
- 225 G/8 OZ VANILLA SUGAR
- 350 G/12 OZ CLEAR FLOWER HONEY
- 175 ML/6 FL OZ WATER OR A FRUITY-FLOWERY DRY WHITE WINE, SUCH AS CHENIN BLANC
- GRATED RIND AND JUICE OF 2 LIMES

Line the pastry tin with pastry

1 Set the oven to 180°C/350°F/Gas 4.

2 For the filling, mix together the nuts, sugar and spices.

Cover with filling

3 Brush a 22.5 × 32 cm/9 × 13 inch baking tin with melted butter, then line the tin with a third of the sheets of phyllo pastry, brushing each sheet with melted butter and pressing the pastry well into the sides and corners of the tin. Cover with half the filling. Repeat the layering once more, using up the rest of the filling, then cover with the remaining pastry sheets. Trim excess pastry with a sharp knife or scissors.

Using a large sharp knife, cut into diamonds

4 Brush the top with melted butter and, with the point of a sharp knife, score approximately 5 cm/2 inch diamonds, to a depth of 1.25 cm/½ inch. Bake for about 1¼–1½ hours until golden and crisp.

5 To make the syrup, gently heat the sugar and honey in the water or wine, stirring with a wooden spoon, until the sugar and honey have dissolved, then bring to the boil without stirring. Boil for 3 minutes. Stir in the lime juice and rind. Leave to cool.

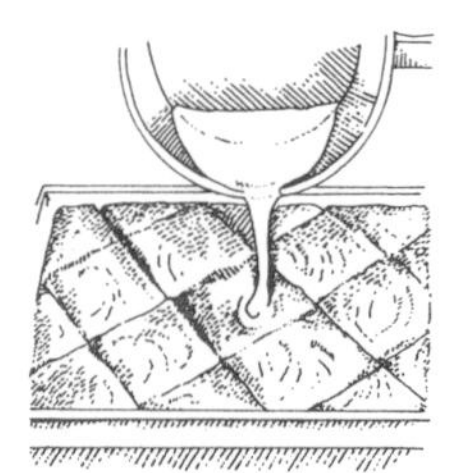

Pour the syrup over the baked baklava

6 Pour the syrup over the baklava as soon as it is taken from the oven and run a fine sharp knife along the score lines so the syrup flows through. Leave to cool in the tin.

7 Just before serving, use a sharp knife to cut right down through the score lines to the bottom of the baklava to separate the number of pieces required. However, try not to eat the baklava too quickly as it continues to improve for up to about 10 days if left in the tin in which it was baked and kept covered in a cool place.

PEAR TART

SERVES 6

This is my favourite pear tart recipe. There seems to be a natural synergy between the melting, light almond pastry, the warm fruitiness of the pears and the contrasting creamy custard with its flavouring of ratafias or amaretti.

- NUT PASTRY MADE WITH 125 G/4½ OZ PLAIN FLOUR, 55 G/2 OZ GROUND BLANCHED ALMONDS, 100 G/3½ OZ UNSALTED BUTTER, 2 EGG YOLKS AND 40 G/1½ OZ ICING SUGAR (SEE PAGE 99)
- 55 G/2 OZ RATAFIA OR ITALIAN AMARETTI BISCUITS
- 2 TBSP *EAU-DE-VIE DE POIRE WILLIAMS*
- 3 RIPE BUT FIRM COMICE OR WILLIAMS PEARS
- 85 G/3 OZ VANILLA CASTER SUGAR
- 2 EGGS, BEATEN
- 175 ML/6 FL OZ DOUBLE CREAM
- ICING SUGAR, FOR SPRINKLING

1 Butter a deep 20 cm/8 inch flan tin. On a lightly floured surface, roll out the pastry and use to line the tin. Prick the base of the pastry case, cover and place in the refrigerator for 30 minutes.

2 Set the oven to 190°C/375°F/Gas 5 and place a baking sheet in the oven.

3 Place the flan tin on the baking sheet and bake the pastry blind for 10 minutes (see page 95). Remove the paper and beans. Return the pastry case to the oven for a further 5 minutes. Leave to cool.

4 Meanwhile, put the ratafia or amaretti biscuits in a small bowl, sprinkle over the eau-de-vie and leave to soak.

5 Peel, halve and core the pears. Put in a saucepan, just cover with water, add the sugar and poach for about 10 minutes until tender. Using a slotted spoon, transfer the pears to absorbent kitchen paper to drain.

6 Stir the eggs and cream into the ratafia or amaretti biscuits.

7 Arrange the pears, cut side down, in the pastry case, then spoon over the cream mixture. Bake for about 35–40 minutes until lightly set. Serve the tart warm sprinkled with icing sugar.

STRAWBERRY CRÈME BRÛLÉE TART

SERVES 6

A real conversation stopper and a sure way to make sure everyone leaves the table with happy memories.

- NUT PASTRY MADE WITH 175 G/6 OZ PLAIN FLOUR, 100 G/3 ½ OZ DICED UNSALTED BUTTER, 2 EGG YOLKS, 1 TBSP KIRSCH (OPTIONAL), 55 G/2 OZ GROUND BLANCHED ALMONDS AND 40 G/1 ½ OZ CASTER SUGAR (SEE PAGE 99)
- APPROXIMATELY 175 G/6 OZ FRESH STRAWBERRIES
- 2 TBSP CASTER SUGAR
- 1 TBSP *EAU-DE-VIE DE FRAMBOISE* OR ORANGE LIQUEUR
- 1 VANILLA POD
- 425 ML/15 FL OZ WHIPPING CREAM
- 4 EGG YOLKS
- CASTER SUGAR, FOR SPRINKLING

1 Butter a 21.5 cm/8½ inch flan tin, which is at least 2.5 cm/1 inch deep. On a lightly floured surface, roll out the nut pastry thinly and use to line the tin. Prick the base of the pastry case, cover and place in the refrigerator for 30 minutes.

2 Cut the strawberries into halves, place in a bowl and sprinkle over 1 tablespoon of sugar and the eau-de-vie or liqueur. Set aside for about 1 hour.

3 Set the oven to 200°C/400°F/Gas 6. Place a baking sheet in the oven.

4 Add the vanilla pod to the cream and heat gently to just below boiling point. Cover, remove from the heat and leave to infuse for 15 minutes.

5 Place the tin on the baking sheet and bake the pastry case blind for 10 minutes (see page 95). Remove the paper and beans, then bake the pastry for a further 12–15 minutes until lightly browned. Transfer to a wire rack to cool completely.

6 In a small bowl, stir together the egg yolks and remaining tablespoon of sugar. Uncover the cream and heat to just below boiling point again. Stir the cream onto the egg yolks, then pour back into the saucepan and heat very gently, stirring with a wooden spoon, until thickened to a smooth custard; do not allow to boil. Pour through a sieve into a bowl and leave to cool, stirring occasionally.

7 Strain off the juices from the strawberries and stir into the custard. Arrange the strawberries in a single layer in the pastry case, then pour over the custard. Smooth the top using a long spatula, then place in the refrigerator for about 2 hours.

8 About 40 minutes before serving, preheat the grill so that it becomes very hot. Sprinkle an even layer of caster sugar, about 5 mm/¼ inch thick, over the entire surface of the custard, taking particular care not to leave any gaps near the pastry. Place the tart close to the grill so that the sugar very quickly melts and becomes golden brown. Chill for 30 minutes.

PEARS IN PYJAMAS

SERVES 4

Crisp, buttery puff pastry makes the perfect covering for warm pears, especially when they contain a surprise in the form of diced dried pear (perhaps soaked in eau-de-vie de poire Williams *or brandy) bound in a marzipan-like mixture in lieu of a core. Alternatively, you could use just a small piece of marzipan or a piece of plain chocolate.*

- 1 QUANTITY PUFF PASTRY (SEE PAGE 100) OR 1 × 375 G/13 OZ PACKET
- BEATEN EGG, FOR GLAZING
- 2 TSP CASTER SUGAR
- **FILLING:**
- 1 DRIED PEAR HALF, CHOPPED (OPTIONAL)
- 2 TBSP *EAU-DE-VIE DE POIRE WILLIAMS*, BRANDY OR WATER (OPTIONAL)
- 4 LARGE DESSERT PEARS, SUCH AS COMICE OR WILLIAMS
- FINELY GRATED RIND AND JUICE OF 1 LEMON
- 115 G/4 OZ GROUND ALMONDS
- 1 EGG YOLK
- **TO SERVE:**
- SINGLE OR WHIPPING CREAM, OR VANILLA DAIRY ICE CREAM

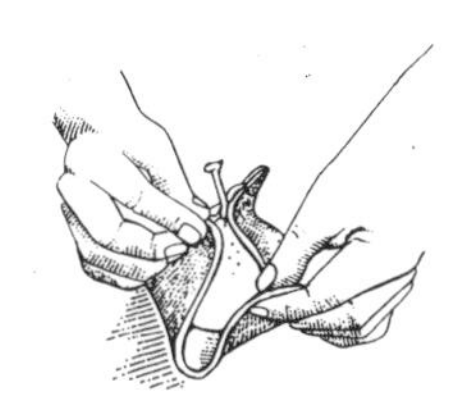

Fold the corners of each pastry square up to the top of each pear

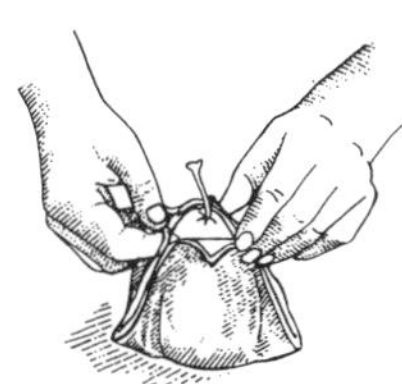

Leave a small opening at the top to allow steam to escape

1 For the filling, soak the dried pear half in the eau-de-vie, brandy or water, if liked, for several hours.

2 On a lightly floured surface, roll out the pastry to just over 35 cm/14 inches square. Using a sharp knife, trim the edges and cut the pastry into four squares. Leave to rest.

3 Peel the pears and core them carefully from the bottom; leave the stalks on. Brush the pears immediately with lemon juice.

4 Mix together the ground almonds and egg yolk, then mix in the dried pear and any remaining soaking liquid, if used. Pack into the cavity in each pear, then stand upright in the centre of each pastry square. Brush the edges of the pastry with water, then fold the four corners up to the top of each pear. Lightly press all the seams and edges to seal, except around the stalk as there must be an outlet for the steam. Stand the pears on the baking sheet and place in the refrigerator for 30 minutes.

5 Set the oven to 220°C/425°F/Gas 7.

6 Brush the pastry with beaten egg and sprinkle with sugar. Bake for 15–20 minutes until the pastry is crisp and golden. Serve warm with single or whipping cream, or vanilla dairy ice cream.

Illustrated opposite page 113

APRICOT AND SESAME PUFFS

SERVES 4–6

These nutty, fruity fried pastries are lighter and less sweet than most. Instead of being soaked in a honey syrup, the syrup is simply poured over the puffs just before they are served; the syrup is also lightened with orange juice.

- 175 G/6 OZ PLAIN FLOUR
- 2½ TSP SESAME SEEDS
- ½ TSP ANISEEDS, FINELY CRUSHED
- 2 TBSP OLIVE OIL
- 25 G/1 OZ UNSALTED BUTTER, MELTED
- 100 ML/3½ FL OZ SWEET WHITE WINE
- APPROXIMATELY 115 ML/4 FL OZ THICK DRIED APRICOT PURÉE
- BEATEN EGG, FOR GLAZING
- SESAME SEEDS, FOR SPRINKLING
- FLAVOURLESS VEGETABLE OIL FOR DEEP FRYING
- **SYRUP:**
- 1 LARGE ORANGE
- 115 ML/4 FL OZ CLEAR HONEY
- 1 TBSP WHISKY OR BRANDY (OPTIONAL)

1 Sieve the flour into a mixing bowl and stir in the sesame seeds and aniseeds. Form a well in the centre. In a saucepan, gently heat together the olive oil, butter and wine until the butter has melted, then slowly pour into the well in the flour mixture, stirring to form a smooth dough. Turn onto a floured surface and knead lightly. Cover and place in the refrigerator for 30 minutes.

2 Roll out the dough thinly and cut into approximately 6.25 cm/2½ inch circles. Place about half a teaspoon of apricot purée on one half of each circle, brush the edges of the dough with water, then fold the uncovered halves over the filling. Press the edges well using a fork or crimping wheel, if liked, to seal. Brush the pastries lightly with beaten egg, then sprinkle with sesame seeds and pat them in lightly.

3 To make the syrup, thinly pare the rind from the orange, then cut into strips. Add to a small saucepan of boiling water, return to the boil then simmer for 2 minutes. Drain and rinse the rind under cold, running water. Squeeze the juice from the orange, then gently heat in a small saucepan with the honey, stirring occasionally with a wooden spoon, until the honey has dissolved. Add the brandy or whisky, if using, and the orange rind. Cover and keep warm over a very low heat.

4 Half fill a deep-fat frying pan with oil, then heat to 180°–190°C/350°–375°F. Fry the pastries in batches for about 3–4 minutes until golden. Using a slotted spoon, transfer to absorbent kitchen paper to drain. When all the puffs are cooked, pile them on a plate and spoon over the honey orange sauce so that all the puffs are coated with sauce.

RIGHT (from top to bottom): Old English Apple Pie (see page 105); Apricot and Sesame Puffs; Caramelized Pineapple Upside-Down Tart (see page 114).

TREACLE TART

SERVES 4–6

The title is a misnomer as treacle tarts do not contain treacle. They used to, until the end of the nineteenth century when the process for refining the thick, black treacle into golden syrup was developed. Traditionally, treacle tarts seem to have been made in old-fashioned pie plates, so the layer of filling was fairly shallow, but this recipe is made in a flan tin to provide a more generous allocation.

- 175 G/6 OZ PLAIN FLOUR
- 85 G/3 OZ UNSALTED BUTTER, DICED
- 1 TBSP CASTER SUGAR
- 1 EGG YOLK
- 2½ TBSP COLD WATER
- 2 TSP FINELY GRATED LEMON RIND
- **FILLING:**
- 225 G/8 OZ GOLDEN SYRUP
- 25 G/1 OZ UNSALTED BUTTER
- GRATED RIND AND JUICE OF 1 LEMON
- 40 G/1½ OZ FRESH BREADCRUMBS
- 40 G/1½ OZ PORRIDGE OATS
- LARGE PINCH OF GROUND CINNAMON OR GINGER (OPTIONAL)
- BEATEN EGG OR MILK, FOR GLAZING

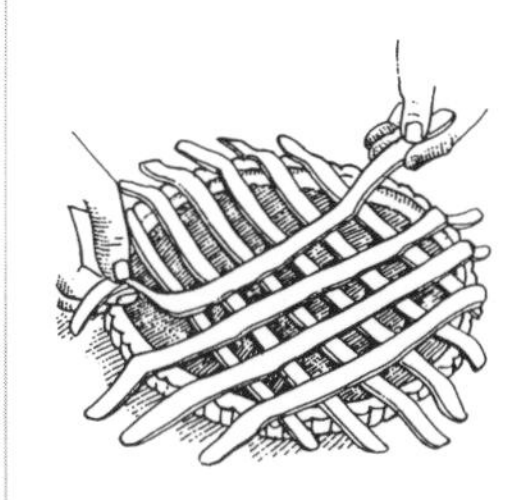

Lay the strips of pastry over the tart to make a lattice pattern

1 Butter a 20 cm/8 inch loose-based flan tin. Place the flour in a bowl, then rub in the butter until the mixture resembles breadcrumbs. Stir in the sugar. Mix the egg yolk with the water and the lemon rind, then lightly and quickly stir into the flour using a fork. Use your hand to quickly form into a ball. On a lightly floured surface, lightly roll out and use to line the tin. Reserve the trimmings. Place the flan tin and trimmings in the refrigerator for 30 minutes.

2 Set the oven to 190°C/375°F/Gas 5.

3 To make the filling, gently warm together the syrup, butter and lemon juice, remove from the heat and stir in the lemon rind, breadcrumbs, oats and cinnamon or ginger, if using.

4 Lightly prick the base of the pastry, taking care not to pierce right the way through. Fill the pastry case with the syrup mixture and level the surface.

5 Roll out the pastry trimmings and cut into strips. Arrange the strips in a lattice pattern over the filling, dampening the ends to seal them to the edge of the pastry case. Brush with beaten egg or milk to glaze.

6 Bake for about 25 minutes until the filling is just set. Serve the tart warm – never hot – or cold.

LEFT (from top to bottom): Treacle Tart; Pears in Pyjamas (see page111); Coconut Cream Pie in a Chocolate Case (see page 126).

CARAMELIZED PINEAPPLE UPSIDE-DOWN TART

SERVES 6

This tart is a development from the French upside-down caramelized apple tart, tarte Tatin, *which in recent years has been in danger of becoming a restaurant cliché. The fresh fruitiness of the pineapple in this version makes a particularly delicious contrast to the sweet buttery topping and they are both well set off by crisp puff pastry. A good accompaniment is lightly sweetened* crème fraîche *or equal quantities of Greek yogurt and sweetened, whipped whipping cream flavoured with a few pieces of finely chopped stem ginger. Alternatively, serve with vanilla dairy ice cream.*

- 115 G/4 OZ UNSALTED BUTTER, DICED
- 115 G/4 OZ LIGHT MUSCOVADO SUGAR
- 1 PINEAPPLE, ABOUT 900 G/2 LB, PEELED, CORED AND SLICED
- PUFF PASTRY MADE WITH 150 G/5 OZ FLOUR AND 150 G/5 OZ UNSALTED BUTTER (SEE PAGE 100)
- KIRSCH (OPTIONAL)
- **DECORATION:**
- FRESH MINT SPRIGS (OPTIONAL)
- **TO SERVE:**
- VANILLA DAIRY ICE CREAM (OPTIONAL)

1 On top of the stove, gently heat the butter in a thick 21.5 cm/8½ inch flan tin or other cake tin such as a *moule à manqué* that is at least 5 cm/2 inches deep. Stir in the sugar using a wooden spoon and heat until it has melted, then continue to cook over a fairly high heat for 3–4 minutes until darkened. Remove from the heat and arrange the pineapple in the sugar-butter mixture. Leave to cool..

2 On a lightly floured surface, roll out the pastry to a 25 cm/10 inch diameter circle. Trim off the edges of the circle. Prick the pastry with a fork and place in the refrigerator for 20–30 minutes.

3 Set the oven to 220°C/425°F/Gas 7. Place a baking sheet in the oven.

4 Place the pastry centrally over the pineapple, tucking the pastry down the side of the tin. Place the tin on the baking tray and bake for 12–15 minutes, then lower the oven temperature to 180°C/350°F/Gas 4 and bake for a further 10–12 minutes until the pastry is well risen and crisp. Run the point of a knife around the edge of the pastry, leave to cool for 2–3 minutes, then place a plate that is larger than the tin over it and invert the two, shaking to unmould the tart. Sprinkle with kirsch, and decorate with mint, if using. Serve with vanilla dairy ice cream, if liked.

Illustrated opposite page 112

BUTTERSCOTCH TART

SERVES 6

To turn this into a classic American butterscotch cream pie, cover the top with a meringue made from two size 2 egg whites and 85 g/3 oz caster sugar and bake at 200°C/400°F/Gas 6 for 8–10 minutes.

- SHORTCRUST PASTRY MADE WITH 175 G/6 OZ PLAIN FLOUR, 115 G/4 OZ UNSALTED BUTTER, 2 TSP VANILLA CASTER SUGAR, 1 EGG YOLK, AND A FEW DROPS OF COLD WATER IF THE DOUGH IS DRY (SEE PAGE 98)
- 1 EGG WHITE
- 55 G/2 OZ UNSALTED BUTTER
- 55 G/2 OZ DARK MUSCOVADO SUGAR
- 150 ML/5 FL OZ MILK
- 3 EGG YOLKS
- 1 EGG
- 1 TBSP CORNFLOUR
- 175 ML/6 FL OZ EVAPORATED MILK
- **TO SERVE:**
- WHIPPED CREAM

1 Butter a 20 cm/8 inch flan tin. On a lightly floured surface, roll out the pastry and use to line the flan tin. Prick the base and place in the refrigerator for 30 minutes.

2 Set the oven to 200°C/400°F/Gas 6. Place a baking sheet in the oven.

3 Place the flan tin on the baking sheet and bake the pastry case blind for 10 minutes (see page 95). Remove the paper and beans, brush the base and sides of the pastry with egg white and return to the oven for 10 minutes. Leave to cool.

4 Meanwhile, in a heavy saucepan, gently melt the butter, then add the sugar and heat until dissolved. Cook for another couple of minutes, then remove from the heat and slowly stir in the milk.

5 In a medium-sized bowl mix together the egg yolks, egg and cornflour, then stir in the milk mixture and the evaporated milk. Return to the saucepan and heat very gently, stirring with a wooden spoon, until thickened. Allow to cool slightly, then pour into the pastry case. Cover the surface of the filling closely with dampened greaseproof paper and leave until cold. Remove the greaseproof paper before serving the tart and serve with whipped cream.

WARM PEACH AND PECAN PIE

SERVES 6

Served warm with crème fraîche *flowing languidly around yielding peaches enlivened with a dash of spirit, and encased in a luxurious pecan pastry, this makes a very special pudding. Barackpálinka is a smooth, Hungarian peach eau-de-vie.*

- NUT PASTRY MADE WITH 225 G/8 OZ PLAIN FLOUR, 55 G/2 OZ PECANS, VERY FINELY CHOPPED, 2 EGG YOLKS, BEATEN, 85 G/3 OZ VANILLA CASTER SUGAR AND 115 G/4 OZ UNSALTED BUTTER, DICED (SEE PAGE 99)
- 1 EGG WHITE, LIGHTLY BEATEN, FOR GLAZING
- CASTER SUGAR, FOR SPRINKLING

FILLING:

- 6 LARGE, RIPE PEACHES
- 1 TBSP VANILLA CASTER SUGAR
- 2 TBSP *EAU-DE-VIE DE PÊCHES*, BARACKPÁLINKA OR COGNAC
- 150 ML/5 FL OZ *CRÈME FRAÎCHE* OR 70 ML/2½ FL OZ DOUBLE CREAM MIXED WITH 70 ML/2½ FL OZ SOURED CREAM

1 Carefully peel the peaches (do this without pouring boiling water over them), then cut into quarters and remove the stones. Slice each quarter in half lengthways. Place in a dish, sprinkle over the sugar and the *eau-de-vie de pêches*, Cognac or Barackpálinka and leave for 1 hour.

2 Butter a 22.5 cm/9 inch loose-based flan tin or flan ring and place on a baking sheet. On a lightly floured surface, roll out the pastry and use about two-thirds to line the tin. Roll the other piece of pastry out to form a lid for the pie. Using an approximately 2.5 cm/1 inch cutter, remove a circle from the centre of the lid. Cover and chill the lined tin and the lid for 30 minutes.

3 Set the oven to 200°C/400°F/Gas 6.

4 Using a slotted spoon, lift the peaches from the dish and arrange the pieces in circles in the pastry case and fill in the centre of the circles with some pieces. Reserve the soaking liquid.

5 Sprinkle a little sugar over the peaches. Dampen the edges of the pastry case and place the lid centrally over the pie. Press the edges together to seal them firmly. Bake for about 20–25 minutes until the pastry is beginning to brown. Brush the top of the pie lightly with beaten egg white, sprinkle with sugar and return to the oven for about 10 minutes until the pastry is browned and crisp. Leave to stand for a few minutes, then remove the sides of the flan tin or the flan ring.

6 Mix together the *crème fraîche*, or double cream and soured cream, and the reserved soaking liquid, then carefully pour through the hole in the lid. Serve warm.

KING-SIZE FIG NEWTON

SERVES 8

A plump pastry bolster, bursting with moist dried fruits to which the addition of an everyday banana gives a hint of the exotic.

- 115 G/4 OZ UNSALTED BUTTER, DICED
- 55 G/2 OZ VANILLA CASTER SUGAR
- 1 EGG, LIGHTLY BEATEN
- 225 G/8 OZ PLAIN FLOUR
- **FILLING:**
- 200 G/7 OZ DRIED FIGS, CHOPPED
- 85 G/3 OZ DRIED APRICOTS, CHOPPED
- 85 G/3 OZ STONED PRUNES, CHOPPED
- 100 G/3½ OZ WALNUTS, CHOPPED
- 40 G/1½ OZ STEM GINGER, FINELY CHOPPED (OPTIONAL)
- 4 TBSP DARK RUM
- 1 LARGE RIPE BANANA
- 1 EGG WHITE, BEATEN
- 150 G/5 OZ ICING SUGAR
- ½ TSP LEMON JUICE
- 2 TBSP APRICOT JAM, SIEVED
- **TO SERVE:**
- CUSTARD (SEE PAGE 181) OR VANILLA DAIRY ICE CREAM

Chop dried fruits with scissors dipped in flour

1 Mix together the figs, apricots, prunes, walnuts, ginger, if using, and the rum for the filling, then leave to soak.

2 Meanwhile, make the pastry. Beat the butter until soft, then beat in the sugar. When well blended, beat in the egg and flour. Cover and place in the refrigerator for 30 minutes.

3 Set the oven to 190°C/375°F/Gas 5. Butter a baking sheet.

4 On a lightly floured surface, roll out the pastry to an approximately 25 cm/10 inch square. Trim the edges. Starting just under 2.5 cm/1 inch in from three sides, spread the dried fruit mixture in a strip almost 10 cm/4 inches wide over the pastry. Peel and slice the banana and lay over the dried fruit mixture.

5 Brush the pastry borders with water, then fold the uncovered dough across the dried fruits. Seal the edges firmly together, then crimp them to make them decorative. If liked, score the top of the pastry to make a diamond pattern, using the point of a sharp knife. Carefully transfer to the baking sheet.

6 In a small bowl, whisk the egg white with the icing sugar until very thick. Stir in the lemon juice, then spread over the top of the pastry. Form a small cone from a 7.5 cm/3 inch square of greaseproof paper, then spoon in the apricot jam. Cut off the tip of the cone and pipe lines of apricot across the egg white coating. Bake for about 20 minutes until golden. Turn off the oven and leave the pastry for a further 15 minutes. If the oven retains the heat very well, leave the door open. Carefully transfer the pastry to a wire rack to cool to room temperature. Cut into slices to serve, accompanied by Custard or vanilla dairy ice cream.

Illustrated opposite page 96

APRICOT TART

SERVES 6

This tart reminds me of summers in the gentle Val de Loire, *where the fertile soil, warm sunshine and blue skies produce rich harvests of flavourful fruit. What bliss to picnic in a grassy spot with a tart such as this one, with its crisp pastry case and buttery custard filling over succulent apricots, and sip a cool glass of a local white wine, such as Vouvray or Côteaux du Layon.*

- *PÂTE SUCRÉE* MADE WITH 175 G/6 OZ PLAIN FLOUR, 100 G/3½ OZ UNSALTED BUTTER, 2 LARGE EGG YOLKS AND 55 G/2 OZ VANILLA CASTER SUGAR (SEE PAGE 99)
- **FILLING:**
- 115 G/4 OZ CASTER SUGAR
- 575 ML/1 PINT WATER
- 550 G/1¼ LB APRICOTS
- 55 ML/2 FL OZ SOURED CREAM
- 175 ML/6 FL OZ DOUBLE CREAM
- ½ VANILLA POD
- 3 EGGS, BEATEN
- 55 G/2 OZ UNSALTED BUTTER, DICED
- CASTER OR ICING SUGAR, FOR SPRINKLING

Lining a fluted flan ring or tin with pastry:

Ease the pastry into the shape of the fluted flan ring or tin

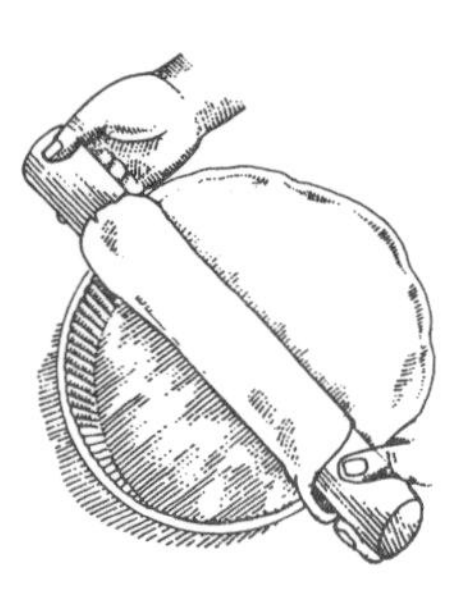

Unroll the pastry over the tin or ring

Use the tin as a guide to the size

1 Butter a 24 cm/9½ inch fluted flan tin, about 2 cm/¾ inch deep, and preferably loose-based. On a lightly floured surface, roll out the pastry and use to line the tin. Prick the base of the pastry case, cover and place in the refrigerator for 30 minutes.

2 Set the oven to 220°C/425°F/Gas 7.

3 Bake the pastry blind (see page 95) for about 12 minutes. Remove the paper and beans, return the pastry to the oven and bake for a further 3–4 minutes. Remove from the oven. Lower the oven temperature to 200°C/400°F/Gas 6.

4 To make the filling, gently heat 85 g/3 oz caster sugar in the water until the sugar has dissolved. Heat to just on simmering point, add the apricots and poach gently until just tender and still retaining their shape (about 5–15 minutes). Drain well and leave on absorbent kitchen paper to drain further.

5 Pour the soured cream and double cream into a saucepan, add the vanilla pod and bring to the boil. In a heatproof bowl, stir together the eggs and remaining caster sugar. Remove the vanilla pod from the saucepan. Slowly pour the boiling liquid onto the egg yolk mixture, stirring constantly, to make a smooth custard. Stir in the butter, then leave to cool, stirring occasionally to prevent a skin forming.

6 Arrange the apricots, cut-side up, in the pastry case, then pour over the custard. Bake for about 20–25 minutes until lightly set in the centre and golden brown.

7 Transfer the flan tin to a wire rack and leave until the tart is lukewarm. Remove the outer ring of the tin, sprinkle the filling with caster or icing sugar and serve.

Black forest puffs

MAKES 6 – 8

This is a new look to the popular combination of cherries and chocolate. You will need to transfer the ice cream to the main part of the refrigerator 20–30 minutes before serving the choux puffs to give it time to soften. The tops of the choux puffs are removed, so you can pile as much ice cream as you like into the shells, but do not fill them until just before serving.

- APPROXIMATELY 225 G/8 OZ STONED RIPE CHERRIES, PREFERABLY BLACK
- 4 TBSP BRANDY OR KIRSCH
- 70 G/2½ OZ PLAIN FLOUR
- 55 G/2 OZ UNSALTED BUTTER, DICED
- 150 ML/5 FL OZ WATER
- 2 EGGS, SIZE 3, BEATEN
- APPROXIMATELY 225–300 ML/8–10 FL OZ VANILLA DAIRY ICE CREAM
- CHOCOLATE SAUCE (SEE PAGE 184)

1 Soak the cherries in the brandy or kirsch for 3 hours.

2 Set the oven to 200°C/400°F/Gas 6. Sprinkle a baking sheet with cold water.

3 Sift the flour onto a piece of paper. In a saucepan, heat the butter in the water until it has just melted, then bring quickly to the boil. Quickly remove from the heat and immediately add all the flour at once and beat vigorously with a wooden spoon until the mixture is smooth and pulls away from the sides of the pan. Return the pan to the heat and beat for 30 seconds. Remove from the heat and allow to cool slightly. Gradually beat in sufficient egg to give a dough that is shiny and soft enough to fall from the spoon.

4 Place 6 or 8 tablespoonfuls of the mixture spaced well apart on the baking sheet, then bake for 10 minutes. Increase the oven temperature to 220°C/425°F/Gas 7 and cook for a further 20–25 minutes until well risen, crisp and golden.

5 Cut a slit in the sides of the buns and, if necessary, return to the oven with the heat turned off for a few minutes to dry out. Transfer to a wire rack to cool completely.

6 Just before serving, cut off the top third or so of each choux bun, place a scoop of ice cream in each bottom portion, then cover with some cherries and spoon the juices over. Cover with the tops and pour over a little warm Chocolate Sauce. Serve the remaining sauce separately.

Illustrated opposite page 96

Gâteau Pithiviers

SERVES 6-8

Uncut, this dome-shaped puff pastry looks fairly innocuous, but remove a slice while it is warm and a rich, melting almond filling will ooze out, languidly and fragrantly, to harmonize beautifully with buttery flakes of crisp pastry. The recipe for the pastry has remained unchanged from at least the beginning of the nineteenth century, and bears the name of a small town about 80 kilometres south of Paris, in the Orleannais.

- Puff Pastry made with 225 g/8 oz plain flour and 225 g/8 oz unsalted butter (see page 100)
- 1 egg yolk beaten with 1 tsp cold water, for glazing
- icing sugar, for sifting

- **FILLING:**
- 85 g/3 oz almonds, ground
- 85 g/3 oz caster sugar
- 85 g/3 oz unsalted butter, softened
- 2 egg yolks, beaten
- 2 tbsp dark rum

1 For the filling, pound the almonds with the sugar to make a paste using a pestle and mortar, then spoon the paste into a bowl and work in the butter followed by the egg yolks and rum. Cover and chill very well.

2 Divide the pastry into two portions, one slightly larger than the other. On a lightly floured surface, roll out the smaller portion, using a lightly floured rolling pin, to a circle about 23.75 cm/9½ inches in diameter. Trim the edges and carefully transfer the pastry to a baking sheet making sure the shape remains true.

3 Roll out the other piece of pastry to a slightly larger circle and trim the edges. Place the almond filling on the first circle, leaving a border of about 2.5 cm/1 inch clear all the way round. Brush the border with egg glaze. Place the second circle of pastry centrally over the filling and press the pastry edges together to seal them. Form a scallop effect around the edge and make a small slit in the centre. With the point of a sharp knife, starting at the centre and working to the edge, score but do not cut right through the surface of the pastry in curved, half-moon shaped lines to give the traditional appearance. Brush the top with egg glaze, avoiding the scored lines. Cover and chill for 30 minutes.

4 Set the oven to 220°C/425°F/Gas 7.

5 Bake the pithiviers for about 20 minutes, then lower the oven temperature to 200°C/400°F/Gas 6 and bake for a further 15 minutes or so until the pastry is risen and golden brown.

6 Set the grill to its highest setting. Sprinkle icing sugar over the surface of the pastry and place under a very hot grill for a minute or two. Carefully transfer to a wire rack to cool slightly.

Illustrated opposite page 96

PECAN PIE

SERVES 6 – 8

Feelings and loyalties run very high on the subject of pecan pie and I would not dare to claim that this is the best, but I do know that it is always declared as being very good. Although walnuts are sometimes substituted for pecans, they have quite a different flavour and texture and will produce a very different pie. Similarly, do not hope to make a proper pecan pie by substituting golden syrup for maple syrup – keep that for using with walnuts.

- *PÂTE SUCRÉE* MADE WITH 200 G/7 OZ PLAIN FLOUR, 115 G/4 OZ BUTTER, 3 SIZE 2 EGG YOLKS, 55 G/2 OZ CASTER SUGAR AND A FEW DROPS OF VANILLA ESSENCE (SEE PAGE 99)
- 300 G/10 OZ PECAN HALVES
- 150 G/5 OZ MAPLE SYRUP
- 175 G/6 OZ SOFT LIGHT BROWN SUGAR
- 1 EGG YOLK
- 3 EGGS, BEATEN
- 1 TBSP DOUBLE CREAM OR MILK
- ½ TSP VANILLA ESSENCE
- 55 G/2 OZ UNSALTED BUTTER, CHOPPED
- **TO SERVE:**
- RUM- OR WHISKY-FLAVOURED WHIPPED CREAM, OR VANILLA DAIRY ICE CREAM

1 Butter a 22.5 cm/9 inch flan tin. On a lightly floured surface, roll out the pastry and use to line the tin. Prick the base and place in the refrigerator for 30 minutes.

2 Set the oven to 200°C/400°F/Gas 6. Place a baking sheet in the oven.

3 Place the flan tin on the baking sheet and bake blind for about 10 minutes (see page 95). Remove the paper and beans and leave to cool.

4 Chop half the pecans and scatter over the bottom of the pastry case.

5 Gently heat together the syrup and sugar, stirring with a wooden spoon, until the sugar has dissolved, then boil for a few minutes. Allow to cool.

6 In a bowl, mix together the egg yolk, eggs, cream or milk and the vanilla essence, then slowly stir in the syrup mixture. Heat the butter in a small saucepan over a medium heat until it turns brown and has a nutty aroma. Pour into the syrup mixture and mix well. Spoon over the chopped nuts, then arrange the pecan halves on top.

7 Bake for 10 minutes, then lower the oven temperature to 170°C/325°F/Gas 3 and bake for a further 25–30 minutes until the centre is just set. Serve warm or cold with rum- or whisky-flavoured whipped cream, or vanilla dairy ice cream.

Tourtière aux pruneaux et Armagnac

SERVES 6

The memory of eating a crisp, flaky, prune-studded tourtière that was heady with Armagnac remained with me long after my return from an eventful trip to the south-west of France, and I made a number of attempts to reproduce it. This is the nearest replica I can make. The tricky part is rolling the dough sufficiently thinly to warrant the traditional French name of voile de mariage *(wedding veil) for this type of pastry. The naming and exact content is also a little difficult to fathom out – the same recipe may be called* croustade *or* pastis *in Gascony,* gâteau Landais *in Bordeaux, where the layers of pastry are sometimes separated by sliced apples instead of prunes sprinkled with Armagnac. To confuse matters further, a* pastis *may have no fruit at all, just a sprinkling of Armagnac. Different sources, all claiming to be authoritative, say contradictory things. Be all that as it may, this is delicious and well worth making.*

- 36 Agen or large prunes
- Armagnac (optional)
- 55 g/2 oz marzipan (optional)
- walnut oil or melted butter, preferably clarified, for greasing
- ½ quantity Puff Pastry (see page 100)
- icing sugar and cornflour sifted together in equal quantities, for sprinkling
- orange flower water
- melted butter, preferably clarified, for brushing
- 1 egg beaten with 1 tsp water, for glazing
- 3 tbsp Armagnac
- icing sugar, for sifting

1 Place the prunes in a saucepan, cover with boiling water and add a few tablespoons of Armagnac, if liked, then leave the prunes to soak for about 2 hours. Bring the saucepan to just below boiling point, remove from the heat and leave to soak again for about 2 hours, by the end of which time the prunes should have softened but retained their shape and the stones be easy to remove. If necessary, repeat the heating again. Remove the stones and, if liked, divide the marzipan between the cavities of twelve of the prunes.

2 Brush a 25 cm/10 inch deep flan tin generously with walnut oil or melted butter.

3 Divide the pastry into five pieces, then form one piece into a ball. Sprinkle the work surface and rolling pin with the icing sugar/cornflour mixture, then roll the ball of pastry out on the work surface thinly to just over 30 cm/12 inches in diameter. Carefully line the tin with the rolled-out pastry. Roll out another piece of pastry in the same way to the same size. Brush the pastry lining the tin with walnut oil or melted butter and cover with the second piece of pastry. Arrange eight of the prunes near the edge of the pastry and place four around the centre. Sprinkle them with a little orange flower water and a little of the icing sugar/cornflour mix. Roll out another piece of pastry in the same way, but this time to 25 cm/10 inches in diameter. Lay this over the prunes, arrange another eight of the marzipan-stuffed prunes, if used, near the edge and four around the centre, placing them in the spaces between the prunes in the layer below. Sprinkle them with a little more orange flower water and sprinkle a little of the cornflour/icing sugar mixture over. Repeat with another portion of pastry and the remaining prunes. Finish with the last piece of pastry and glaze with beaten egg. Fold the edges of the first two layers of pastry down over the top. Cover and place in the refrigerator for 30 minutes.

4 Set the oven to 220°C/425°F/Gas 7.

5 Brush the top of the tourtière well with melted butter and bake for about 10 minutes, then reduce the oven temperature to 200°C/400°F/Gas 6 and bake for a further 20 minutes or so until the top is crisp and golden. Carefully transfer the tourtière to a wire rack, cut a small hole in the centre and pour in the Armagnac, rolling the tin from side to side so all the parts receive some. Sift icing sugar over the top and serve lukewarm.

St Clements Tart

SERVES 6

In Britain, the name St Clements signifies the combination of oranges and lemons, after the old nursery rhyme 'Oranges and Lemons'. Here, they harmonize beautifully to make a welcomely refreshing tart. If your oven tends to be on the hot side, reduce the temperature further when cooking the filling, otherwise it may bubble over or colour too quickly.

- *PÂTE SUCRÉE* MADE WITH 125 G/4½ OZ FLOUR, 70 G/2½ OZ BUTTER, 2 EGG YOLKS AND 25 G/1 OZ CASTER SUGAR (SEE PAGE 99)
- 1 EGG WHITE, LIGHTLY BEATEN
- 3 EGGS, SIZE 3
- 1 EGG YOLK, SIZE 3
- 175 G/6 OZ CASTER SUGAR
- FINELY GRATED RIND AND STRAINED JUICE OF 2 ORANGES AND 1 LEMON
- 150 ML/5 FL OZ *CRÈME FRAÎCHE* OR DOUBLE CREAM
- **DECORATION:**
- 1 THIN SKINNED LEMON
- 1 SMALL ORANGE
- 175 G/6 OZ CASTER SUGAR
- 115 ML/4 FL OZ WATER

1 For the decoration, pare the rind very thinly from half of the orange and half of the lemon using a potato peeler, making sure that none of the white pith is included. Cut the rind into very fine shreds, then blanch three times, using fresh water each time and rinsing well after each blanching. Drain. Gently heat 70 g/2½ oz of the sugar in the water, stirring with a wooden spoon, until the sugar has dissolved, then bring to the boil without stirring. Add the orange and lemon shreds and simmer very gently until they are tender and translucent. Remove from the syrup and leave to drain on a wire rack.

2 Meanwhile, peel the lemon and the orange, making sure that all the pith has been removed, then divide into segments. Gently heat the remaining sugar in 200 ml/7 fl oz water, stirring with a wooden spoon, until the sugar has dissolved, then bring to the boil without stirring. Reduce the heat so the syrup barely simmers, then lower in the orange and lemon segments using a slotted spoon and cook gently for about 3–4 minutes. Lift from the syrup using a slotted spoon and leave to drain on a wire rack placed over a tray.

3 Butter a deep 20 cm/8 inch flan tin. On a lightly floured surface, roll out the pastry and use to line the tin. Prick the base, cover and chill for 30 minutes.

4 Set the oven to 200°C/400°F/Gas 6.

5 Bake the pastry case blind (see page 95) for 10 minutes. Remove the paper and beans, brush the base of the tart with beaten egg white, then leave the pastry case to cool to room temperature.

6 Lower the oven temperature to 150°C/300°F/Gas 2.

7 Blend the eggs and egg yolk with the sugar until it has dissolved, then beat in the fruit juices and rinds and the *crème fraîche* or cream. With the tart shell still in the flan ring and on a baking tray, pour in most of the filling. Carefully place the baking tray on an oven shelf and spoon in the remaining filling. Slide the oven shelf into position and bake for about 25–30 minutes until the filling is just set (test it by shaking it gently). Leave to stand for several minutes before transferring to a wire rack to cool. Decorate the tart with the orange and lemon segments and shreds.

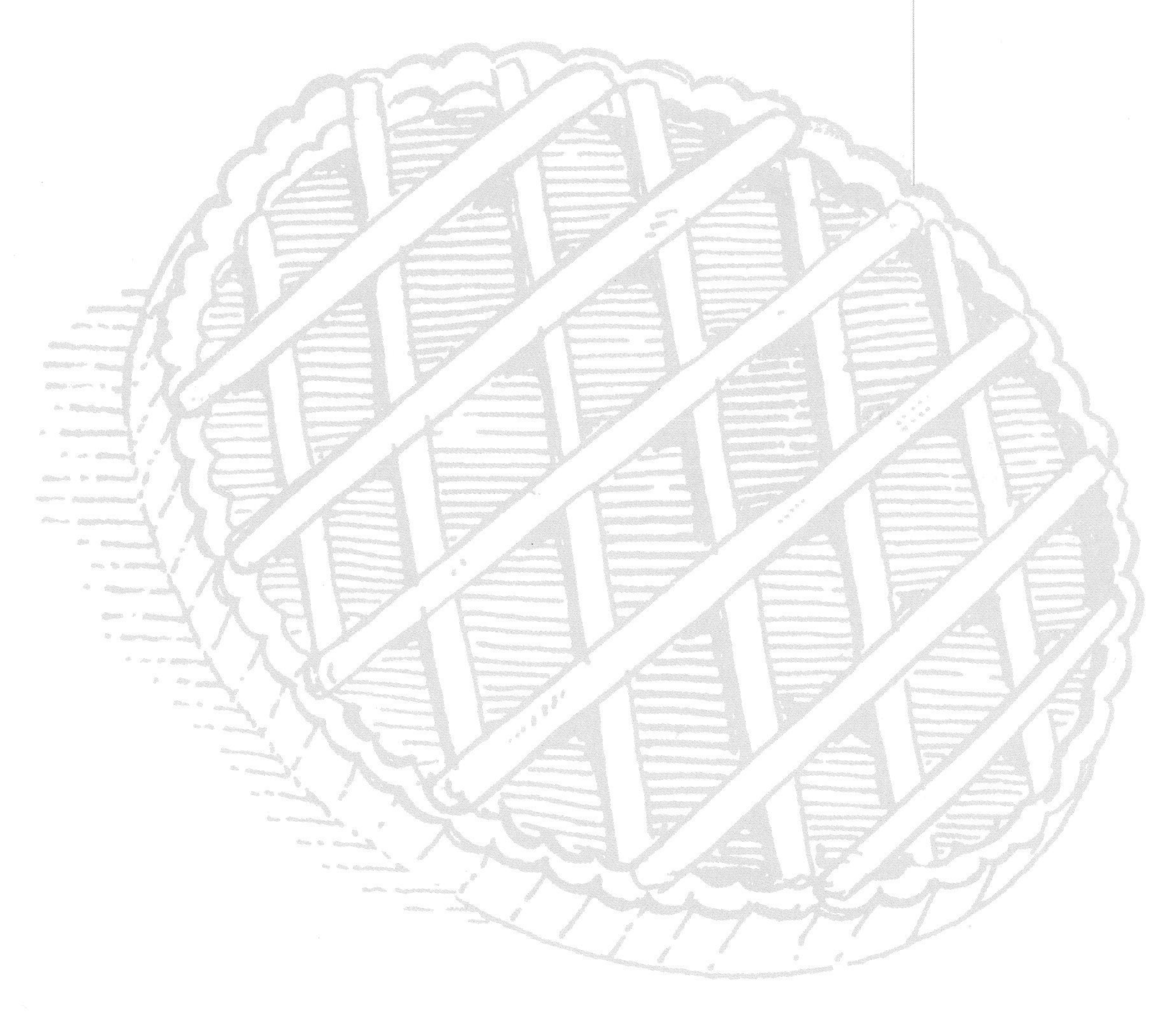

Coconut cream pie in a chocolate case

SERVES 8–10

This is not an American 'cream pie' (those do not actually contain cream, but a cooked custard put into a cooked pastry case), but one with coconut-flavoured cream baked in a shell of chocolate pastry so that the two fuse harmoniously together. Nestling on the pastry, surrounded by the coconut cream, a few rum-soaked cherries provide a final highlight.

- **CHOCOLATE PASTRY:**
- 175 G/6 OZ PLAIN FLOUR
- 2 TBSP COCOA POWDER
- 4 TBSP VANILLA ICING SUGAR OR ORDINARY ICING SUGAR PLUS 2 OR 3 DROPS VANILLA ESSENCE
- 115 G/4 OZ UNSALTED BUTTER, DICED
- 1 TBSP WATER
- 1 EGG WHITE, BEATEN
- **FILLING:**
- 176 G/6 OZ RIPE CHERRIES, HALVED AND STONED
- 3 TBSP WHITE RUM
- 70 G/2½ OZ SOLID COCONUT CREAM, CHOPPED
- 500 ML/18 FL OZ SINGLE, WHIPPING OR DOUBLE CREAM, OR A MIXTURE
- 2 EGGS, BEATEN
- 4 EGG YOLKS
- APPROXIMATELY 100 G/3½ OZ CASTER SUGAR
- **DECORATION:**
- LIGHTLY TOASTED FLAKED COCONUT

1 Butter a 25 cm/10 inch deep loose-based flan tin. For the filling, leave the cherries to marinate in the rum. Put the coconut cream into a bowl. In a saucepan, gently warm the cream, pour over the coconut cream and leave until cold, stirring occasionally to dissolve the coconut.

2 To make the pastry, sift the flour, cocoa powder and icing sugar into a bowl. In a saucepan, gently heat the butter with the water until the butter has just melted, then slowly pour onto the flour mixture, stirring with a wooden spoon to make a smooth dough. Transfer to the flan tin and press evenly into the shape. Cover and place in the refrigerator for 30 minutes.

3 Set the oven to 190°C/375°F/Gas 5.

4 Bake the pastry case blind for 10 minutes (see page 95), remove the paper and beans, brush the pastry case with egg white and return to the oven for about 5 minutes. Remove from the oven and leave to cool.

5 Lower the oven temperature to 170°C/325°F/Gas 3.

6 To make the filling, strain the liquid from the cherries into a bowl and arrange the cherries, cut side down, in the pastry case.

7 Add the eggs, egg yolks, sugar and coconut cream mixture to the bowl and stir together. Pour into the tin and bake for about 50 minutes until lightly set in the centre. Leave to cool, then carefully transfer to a wire rack to cool completely. Serve sprinkled with flaked coconut.

Illustrated opposite page 113

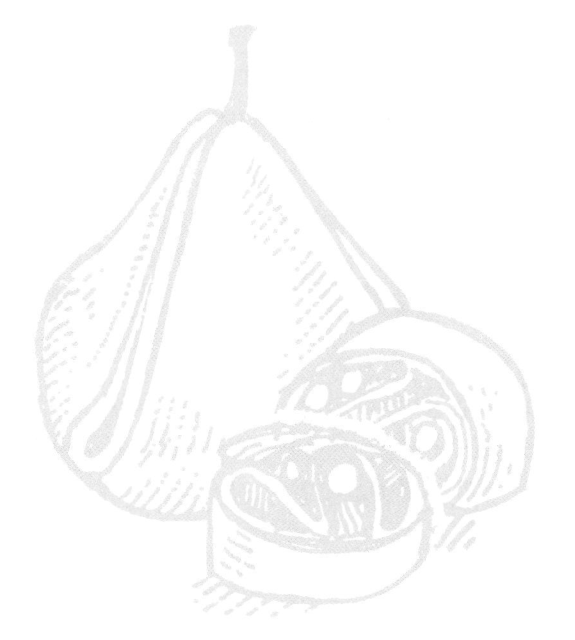

WALNUT TARTLETS

SERVES 8

If current thinking is correct, walnuts help to lower cholesterol levels in the blood, so as these tartlets are packed with them, they might help to negate the effect of the butter and cream (but dietary and nutritional claims do seem to be prone to being revoked). If calories are your concern, sorry, there is nothing that can ease the impact on your figure of each delicious mouthful, so the best thing is to forget them altogether and simply enjoy this wonderful pudding.

- 100 G/3½ OZ FULL-FAT SOFT CHEESE
- 100 G/3½ OZ UNSALTED BUTTER, DICED
- 1 EGG YOLK
- 115 G/4 OZ PLAIN FLOUR
- **FILLING:**
- 175 G/6 OZ LIGHT MUSCOVADO SUGAR
- FEW DROPS LEMON JUICE
- 2 TBSP WATER
- 55 ML/2 FL OZ DOUBLE CREAM
- 175 G/6 OZ UNSALTED BUTTER, DICED
- FEW DROPS VANILLA ESSENCE
- 225 G/8 OZ WALNUT HALVES
- **TO SERVE:**
- ICED MASCARPONE (SEE PAGE 80) OR VANILLA DAIRY ICE CREAM

1 Put the cheese, butter and egg yolks in a mixing bowl and beat together until evenly combined, then gradually mix in the flour. Cover and place in the refrigerator for 30 minutes.

2 On a lightly floured surface and using a lightly floured rolling pin, roll out the pastry thinly and use to line eight approximately 7.5 cm/3 inch fluted tartlet tins. Prick the base of each case, then place in the refrigerator for about 30 minutes.

3 Set the oven to 190°C/375°F/Gas 5. Place a baking sheet in the oven.

4 Place the tins on the baking sheet and bake blind (see page 95) for 10 minutes. Remove the paper and beans and return the pastry to the oven for 5 minutes.

5 To make the filling, gently heat the sugar and lemon juice in a heavy-based saucepan with the water until the sugar has melted, then increase the heat and boil until lightly caramelized. Remove from the heat and quickly add the cream, which will bubble a lot. Swirl the pan gently until the bubbles subside, then stir in the butter, vanilla essence and nuts.

6 Divide between the pastry cases and return to the oven for 10 minutes.

7 Leave to cool on a wire rack for a few minutes, then slip them out of the tins on to plates. Serve warm with Iced Mascarpone or vanilla dairy ice cream.

RIGHT (from top to bottom): Tangerine Syllabub (see page 161); Paskha (see page 146); Orange-Flavoured Babas with Kumquats (see page 168).

Illustrated opposite page 97

What Went Wrong?

SHORTCRUST, PATE SUCREE AND PUFF PASTRY

☞ **PASTRY BECOMES STICKY:**
There are three reasons for this. The dough may have become too warm, because the ingredients or equipment are warm, the atmosphere in the kitchen is warm or your hands are warm; too much water may have been added; or you have been too heavy-handed.

☞ **TOUGH PASTRY:**
Too much water added to the dough and rough handling are the culprits.

☞ **PASTRY SHRINKS AFTER BAKING:**
This is caused by too much water being added when making the dough, and/or the dough being overstretched when rolled out, and/or the dough not being allowed to rest before baking.

☞ **FAT RUNS OUT DURING BAKING:**
The oven was too cool or too much fat was added to the dough.

☞ **SOGGY PASTRY BENEATH A FILLING:**
If the pastry has not been baked blind, or sealed with beaten egg white before being filled, or sugar comes into contact with the pastry, it will be soggy.

CHOUX PASTRY

☞ **THE DOUGH IS TOO SOFT:**
The dough will be too soft if it was not allowed to cool sufficiently between adding the flour and beating in the eggs.

☞ **THE PASTRY DOES NOT RISE:**
If the dough was too soft or the oven was not hot enough the pastry will not rise.

☞ **UNCOOKED DOUGH INSIDE THE BAKED PASTRY:**
This is caused by insufficient baking, failure to pierce a hole in the pastry to allow the steam to escape and not returning the pastry to the oven to dry out.

LEFT (from top to bottom): Banana Butterscotch Sundae (see page 149); Brown Sugar Meringues with Egg Nog Parfait and Orange Compote (see page 158); Italian Coffee Cream and Walnut Cake (see page 165).

COLD PUDDINGS

CHAPTER FIVE

An advantage of serving cold puddings is that, with a few exceptions, they can be made in advance so are ready and waiting for you when you are ready for them, saving last-minute preparation, cooking and worry. Cold puddings should not be thought of as only warm-weather fare, because there are many that are as suitable for eating around a blazing open fire as when basking under a hot sun. The range is vast and varied. It includes luscious cake-type recipes; traditional dishes often associated with the nursery but nevertheless evocative and, when made well, delicious, such as honeycombe moulds and blancmange; ever-popular ice cream-based puddings; and old-fashioned favourites such as fools and trifles that never seem to lose their appeal.

COLD PUDDINGS

GELATINE

☞ There are two forms of gelatine that can be used to set puddings, the more common powdered type sold weighed out in sachets and the less widely available brittle, transparent leaf or sheet gelatine.
☞ The amount of gelatine required will vary depending on the firmness of the set required, the density of the mixture and the temperature of the surroundings. As a general rule, in Britain one sachet of powdered gelatine, which is usually 3–4 teaspoons, will set 550 ml/1 pint of liquid. Leaf gelatine should be weighed, as different brands may have different weights, so check the packet to find how many sheets are needed for a given volume of liquid.
☞ Gelatine sets at 20°C/68°F and is at its best if not left in the refrigerator for more than a few hours as it will become very firm.
☞ Cover the dish while a pudding containing gelatine is in the refrigerator.

Place the bowl over a saucepan of hot water

TO USE GELATINE

POWDERED GELATINE:
☞ The gelatine must be 'sponged' in a small amount of water in a small heatproof bowl first. To do this, sprinkle the gelatine over the water, usually about 3 tablespoons water for 1 tablespoon or 1 sachet gelatine, and leave until the gelatine has swollen to resemble a sponge in appearance; this takes about 5 minutes.
☞ The gelatine must then be dissolved completely. Place the bowl over a saucepan of hot, not boiling, water, leave for 5 minutes, then stir with a teaspoon. Leave until the liquid is clear.
☞ Do not add hot gelatine to a cold mixture, otherwise it will set quickly into unpleasant, rubbery strings. Remove the bowl from the saucepan, leave the gelatine to cool, then slowly stir a little of the cold mixture into the dissolved gelatine. This can then be slowly poured back into the remaining mixture, stirring constantly.

Squeeze sheets of gelatine to remove excess water

LEAF GELATINE:
☞ Soak the required number of leaves in a small amount of water for about 5 minutes or until very soft, then remove from the water and squeeze out excess moisture. Put the leaves in a small heatproof bowl, usually about 3 leaves of gelatine to 3 tablespoons water, place the bowl over a saucepan of hot, not boiling, water and proceed as for powdered gelatine.

WORKING WITH CHOCOLATE

Melt chocolate in a double saucepan

☞ For advice on the choice of chocolate see page 11.
☞ If chocolate is heated to too high a temperature or for too long it will become granular when other ingredients are added.
☞ To melt chocolate, chop it, then place in a heatproof bowl placed over a saucepan of hot water; check that the underside of the bowl is not touching the water. Leave until the chocolate has melted around the edges, stir and leave until completely

melted. Remove from the heat.
☞ Steam and water can make chocolate thick and unmanageable. Should this happen, gradually stir in a little flavourless oil until the mixture is smooth.
☞ The same remedy can be used to rescue chocolate that has been overheated.
☞ Combine melted chocolate while it is warm with ingredients that are at a similar temperature. If they are much hotter or colder the chocolate may turn lumpy.

SUCCESSFUL MERINGUES

☞ Fat and water inhibit egg whites from being beaten to a stiff foam, so the bowl and whisk should be clean and dry.
☞ The temperature of the ingredients is not vital to the success of the meringue, but if the egg whites are at room temperature rather than at refrigerator temperature they will be easier to whisk to a foam.
☞ The proportion of sugar that is added determines the final texture of the meringue – 2 tablespoons of sugar per egg white produces a soft meringue, 4 tablespoons per egg white a hard one. Sugar helps to protect the meringue from drainage and collapse, but it also reduces the foaming of the egg whites, so it should not be added until the final stages of the whisking.
☞ For more than two centuries, the use of a copper bowl has been recommended for whisking egg whites because it produces a good creamy foam that is more difficult to overbeat, but just why this should be so remains a mystery. Theories that the copper gives acidity to the whites or that it establishes an electric field have not been substantiated.
☞ The addition of a small amount of an acid, such as a pinch of cream of tartar or a few drops of lemon juice or a mild vinegar, help to guard against overbeating and the overcoagulation of the egg whites, which results in lumpiness, collapse of the meringue and seeping of liquid.
☞ Although salt enhances the flavour of foods, it should not be added to meringues; it increases the time required to whisk the eggs to a foam and it decreases the stability.

Making meringues:

Whisk the egg whites until soft peaks form

Using a large metal spoon, gently fold in the sugar

STORING COLD PUDDINGS

Puddings containing cream, milk, uncooked eggs, such as whips and mousses, and gelatine should be kept cool and eaten within a day of being made, or less if they do have to be left in a warm room. Puddings that can be refrigerated can be kept for a day longer, but they must be covered while in the refrigerator and usually should be returned to room temperature before being eaten. However, they will lose much of their former glory.

PASSION FRUIT WHIP

SERVES 4

The hard, wrinkled shell of the passion fruit belies the intense, refreshing perfume of the translucent pulp that clings to the small, crunchy seeds inside. Combined with orange, which enhances, and therefore 'stretches', its flavour, passion fruit makes a simple fruit pudding that will remind you of far-away, sunny places.

- 12 PASSION FRUITS
- 2 TBSP COINTREAU
- 6 TBSP VANILLA ICING SUGAR
- 250 ML/9 FL OZ WHIPPING CREAM, WHIPPED
- 2 EGG WHITES, SIZE 2

TO SERVE:

- SHORTBREAD BISCUITS

1 Cut the passion fruit in half and scoop the insides into a saucepan. Heat gently, then tip into a non-metallic sieve and push the flesh through into a bowl; reserve a few of the seeds for decoration. Add the Cointreau to the passion fruit flesh and leave at room temperature for about 1 hour.

2 Stir the icing sugar into the passion fruit, then, using a cold metal spoon, fold in the cream. Cover and place in the refrigerator for 1 hour or more.

3 Just before serving, in a clean, dry bowl, whisk the egg whites until stiff but not dry, then, using a large metal spoon, gently fold into the passion fruit mixture. Spoon into chilled glasses and decorate with the reserved passion fruit seeds. Serve with shortbread biscuits.

APRICOT ROULADE

SERVES 8

A friend who knows how much I like dried apricots suggested the basic idea for this pudding to me after she had been served a similar pudding at a dinner party. And what a good idea. The rich fruit flavour of good dried apricots wrapped around a cool, creamy filling is given just the right 'lift' by strained Greek yogurt. It makes the sort of end to a meal that I can't wait to reach.

- 450 G/1 LB TRADITIONAL DRIED APRICOTS, SOAKED OVERNIGHT
- FINELY GRATED RIND OF 1 LARGE ORANGE
- 4 EGGS, SIZE 2, SEPARATED
- 115 G/4 OZ DEMERARA SUGAR
- ICING SUGAR, FOR SIFTING

FILLING:

- 115 ML/4 FL OZ STRAINED GREEK YOGURT
- 115 ML/4 FL OZ DOUBLE CREAM, LIGHTLY WHIPPED

1 Simmer the apricots in their soaking liquor with the orange rind until tender, increasing the heat towards the end of the cooking to drive off excess moisture.

2 Set the oven to 180°C/350°F/Gas 4. Line a 30 × 35 cm/12 × 14 inch Swiss roll tin with non-stick silicone paper.

3 Drain and reserve the last drops of juice from the apricots, then purée them with the orange rind. Add 3 tablespoons of the purée to the juice and put this to one side for the filling.

4 Whisk the egg yolks with half the sugar until thick and pale.

5 In a clean, dry bowl, whisk the egg whites until soft peaks form, then gradually whisk in the remaining sugar, whisking well after each addition, until the mixture is stiff and shiny. Using a large metal spoon, very gently fold into the egg yolk mixture in four batches, adding the apricot purée at the same time. Spoon evenly into the tin and bake for 20–25 minutes until well risen and pale golden brown.

6 Lay a sheet of non-stick silicone paper over the roulade and cover that with a damp tea towel. Leave to cool.

7 To make the filling, beat the yogurt, then stir in the reserved apricot purée and juice. Lightly fold in the double cream.

8 To finish the cake, sift icing sugar over a sheet of non-stick silicone paper, then invert the roulade onto it. Carefully peel away the lining paper, tearing it in strips to avoid tearing the cake. Spread the cream mixture over the roulade, then roll it up lengthways. Carefully transfer to a serving dish and sift over more icing sugar.

Lining a cornered tin:

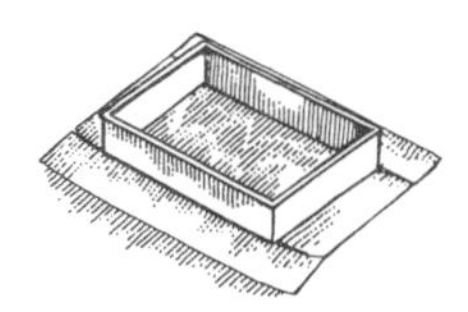

Use the tin as a guide to cut a paper piece, larger all round

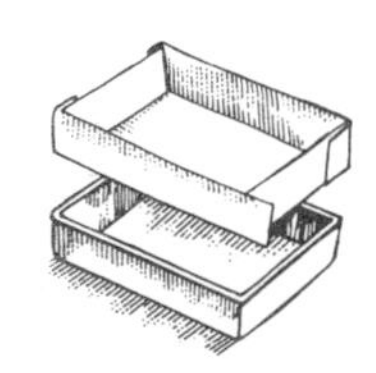

Fold the edges up around the tin, then fit snugly inside

Peeling chestnuts:

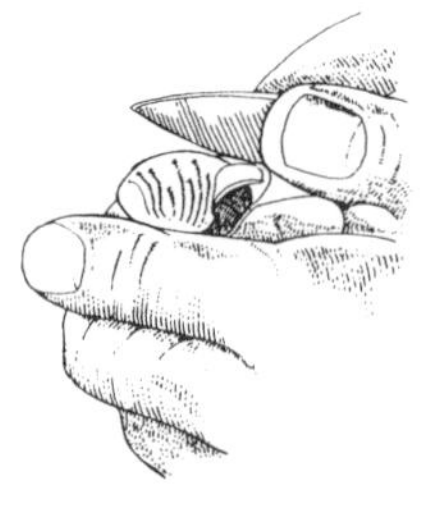

Peel off the thick outer skin

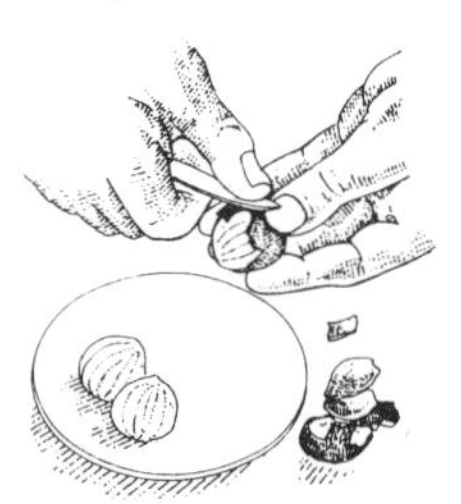

Peel and scrape off the thin, inner skin

CHESTNUT COMPOTE WITH COFFEE SAUCE

SERVES 4 – 6

Fresh chestnuts are set off by the rich, dark, coffee-flavoured sauce to make a wonderful pudding. Do not spoil the effect by using canned or reconstituted nuts. I always buy bagfuls of fresh nuts around Christmas and freeze them, both in and out of their shells, so that I will be able to make recipes such as this during at least some of the rest of the year. Peeling chestnuts can be a little fiddly, but if you do it while the nuts are hot or warm, the shell and skin should be quite easy to remove. It is a good idea to have a few spare nuts to hand in case some are bad, although I have not found this a problem with chestnuts sold by supermarkets.

- APPROXIMATELY 32 CHESTNUTS (PLUS A FEW EXTRA AS A PRECAUTION)
- 55 G/2 OZ SUGAR
- 300 ML/10 FL OZ WATER
- 1 VANILLA POD

COFFEE SAUCE:

- 3 EGG YOLKS
- 3 TBSP VANILLA CASTER SUGAR, TO TASTE
- 100 ML/3½ FL OZ STRONG BLACK COFFEE, PREFERABLY ESPRESSO

1 Cut a cross through the outer skin of the rounded side of each chestnut, then place in a saucepan of boiling water. Leave for about 2–3 minutes. Remove the pan from the heat, remove some of the nuts and peel off both the outer shell and the inner skin. Repeat until all the nuts have been peeled. If any nuts cool before they are peeled, return them to the hot water to warm again.

2 Gently heat the sugar in the water, stirring with a wooden spoon, until the sugar has dissolved. Bring to the boil, add the vanilla pod and the chestnuts and simmer for about 30 minutes until tender. Leave to cool in the liquid, then divide between 4 small serving dishes or glasses.

3 To make the sauce, place the egg yolks, sugar and coffee in a heatproof bowl, place over a saucepan of hot water and whisk until foamy and almost thick enough to support a trail of the mixture. Remove from the heat and continue to whisk for about 1 minute. Transfer to a warmed serving bowl.

Illustrated opposite page 145

Blueberry Cloud

SERVES 4

The covering for the plump blue-black berries has just the right combination of lightness and creaminess that you neither feel as if you are eating mouthfuls of nothing, nor as if you are eating something so rich you might regret it. Cultivated blueberries are imported from North America both fresh and frozen; they freeze well, so if you are unable to find fresh berries, look in the freezer cabinet. Blueberries are also cultivated in Britain on a small scale.

- 350–450 G/12 OZ–1 LB BLUEBERRIES
- 225 ML/8 FL OZ SOURED CREAM
- 70 G/2½ OZ CASTER SUGAR
- 175 G/6 OZ CREAM CHEESE
- 2 EGGS, SIZE 2, SEPARATED
- FEW DROPS ALMOND ESSENCE
- 1 EGG WHITE
- 2 TBSP FLAKED ALMONDS
- 2 TBSP ICING SUGAR

1 Set the oven to 190°C/375°F/Gas 5. Butter a 1.2 litre/2 pint ovenproof dish and put the blueberries in the bottom.

2 Stir the soured cream and half the sugar into the cream cheese, then beat until light and fluffy. Beat in the egg yolks and a few drops of almond essence to make a thick, light mixture.

3 In a clean bowl, whisk the egg whites until soft peaks form, then gradually whisk in the remaining sugar, whisking well after each addition, until the mixture is stiff and shiny. Using a large metal spoon, gently fold into the cream cheese mixture, then pour over the blackberries.

4 Bake for about 35–40 minutes until risen and lightly set in the centre. Preheat the grill on the highest setting.

5 Sprinkle flaked almonds and icing sugar over the top of the pudding and place under the hot grill until golden. Leave to cool and serve at room temperature.

Divide the caramel between the dishes and immediately swirl it around to coat the base and sides

TANGY
ORANGE CARAMELS

SERVES 4

The bitter taste of the caramel topping both contrasts with and complements the tang and texture of the smooth orange custard. Whether you squeeze the oranges yourself, or buy freshly-squeezed juice from a supermarket, really well-flavoured juice will make all the difference.

- GRATED RIND OF 1 ORANGE
- 300 ML/10 FL OZ ORANGE JUICE
- 3 WHOLE EGGS
- 3 EGG YOLKS
- 2 TBSP CASTER SUGAR

CARAMEL:
- 115 G/4 OZ CASTER SUGAR
- 1 TBSP WATER

1 Add the orange rind to the orange juice and leave to soak.

2 Set the oven to 180°C/350°F/Gas 4. Warm 4 ramekin dishes.

3 To make the caramel, in a small, heavy-based saucepan, gently heat the sugar in the water, swirling the pan, until the sugar has dissolved, then cook until golden brown. Immediately pour a quarter into each dish and swirl them around so that the caramel coats the sides and base. Place in a baking tin.

4 Gently heat the orange juice and orange rind until just below simmering point.

5 Meanwhile, whisk the whole eggs and egg yolks with the sugar until thick, then slowly pour in the orange juice, whisking constantly. Divide between the dishes, then pour boiling water around them. Cover the dishes with greaseproof paper and cook for about 25 minutes until lightly set.

6 Remove the dishes from the baking tin and leave until cold.

7 Unmould the puddings just before serving. To do this, place a plate over each dish, hold the plate and dish firmly together, invert them and give a sharp shake. Carefully lift off the dish.

CHOCOLATE TRUFFLE LOAF

SERVES 6–8

This is very rich – ambrosia for chocoholics, and very good for many other people as well. As it contains protein, vitamins A, B_1 (thiamine), B_2 (riboflavin), B_3 (niacin), D, E and K, iron and calcium, this pudding could also be construed as quite nutritious! If you would like to 'dilute' the richness, line the terrine, tin or basin with sponge cake before filling with the chocolate mixture.

- 300 ML/10 FL OZ WHIPPING OR DOUBLE CREAM
- 1 VANILLA POD
- 300 G/10 OZ PLAIN CHOCOLATE, CHOPPED
- 1 TBSP INSTANT COFFEE GRANULES
- 2 TBSP COGNAC
- 1 TBSP WATER
- 55 G/2 OZ UNSALTED BUTTER, CHOPPED
- 4 EGG YOLKS, SIZE 2

DECORATION:

- COCOA POWDER, FOR SIFTING
- WHIPPED CREAM
- GRATED PLAIN CHOCOLATE

TO SERVE:

- COLD CUSTARD (SEE PAGE 181) OR SINGLE CREAM

1 Slowly heat the cream and vanilla pod to just on simmering point, cover, remove from the heat and leave until cold.

2 Place the chocolate, coffee granules, Cognac and the water in a heatproof bowl placed over a saucepan of hot water and leave, stirring occasionally, until melted and smooth. Remove the bowl from the heat and leave to cool slightly.

3 Beat the butter and egg yolks together until pale and fluffy, then, using a large, metal spoon, gently fold in the chocolate mixture.

4 Strain the cream and whip until soft peaks form. Using a large metal spoon, gently fold into the chocolate mixture.

5 Line a 850 ml–1.2 litre/1½–2 pint terrine, loaf tin or freezer-proof basin with cling film. Spoon in the chocolate mixture, smooth the surface and place in the freezer for about 2 hours until firm but not frozen.

6 Unmould the pudding, carefully remove the cling film, sift over cocoa powder and decorate with whipped cream and grated plain chocolate. Serve with cold Custard or single cream.

Illustrated opposite page 17

FORGOTTEN LEMON HEAVEN

SERVES 6

I acquired this recipe when I was at college in the mid-sixties and it was so popular that it became the standard pudding for special occasions when I was sharing a flat in London, at home in the country and when I was first married. Then, as I entertained more, I moved on to other recipes and forgot about this one, until recently. Suddenly, I thought about the wonderful lemon flavour, the smooth texture and how it tasted so very special without being too rich. I could not remember, though, having seen the distinctive card in the kitchen for years. But within about 1 minute, to my extreme surprise, I came across it. I did not doubt that the reality would be as good as the memory. And I was right. As the first spoonful melted in my mouth, a whole host of memories flooded back.

- 4 TBSP WATER
- 3 TSP POWDERED GELATINE
- FINELY GRATED RIND AND JUICE OF 2 LEMONS
- 3 EGGS, SEPARATED
- 115 G/4 OZ CASTER SUGAR
- 150 ML/5 FL OZ SINGLE CREAM
- 350 G/12 OZ COTTAGE CHEESE, SIEVED
- 150 ML/5 FL OZ DOUBLE CREAM, LIGHTLY WHIPPED

CRUST:

- 8 DIGESTIVE BISCUITS, CRUSHED
- 25 G/1 OZ DEMERARA SUGAR
- 55 G/2 OZ UNSALTED BUTTER, MELTED

DECORATION:

- CRYSTALLIZED LEMON SLICES

1 Lightly brush the sides and bottom of a 20 cm/8 inch loose-based springform cake tin with a flavourless vegetable oil.

2 To make the crust, mix the ingredients together, then spoon evenly over the base of the tin and press down lightly.

3 Place the water into a small heatproof bowl, sprinkle the gelatine over the top and leave for about 5 minutes until the gelatine becomes spongy.

4 Meanwhile, place the lemon rind, egg yolks and sugar in a mixing bowl and whisk together until pale and thick enough to support a trail of mixture when the beaters are lifted.

5 When the gelatine has become spongy, place the bowl over a saucepan of hot water and leave until the gelatine has melted, stirring occasionally. Remove the bowl from the heat and allow to cool slightly.

6 Stir a little of the single cream into the gelatine, then stir in the remaining single cream.

7 Put the cottage cheese into a bowl and stir in the single cream and lemon juice. Using a large metal spoon, lightly fold into the egg yolk mixture and leave until thick but not quite set.

8 In a clean, dry bowl, whisk the egg whites until stiff but not dry, then, using a large metal spoon, lightly fold into the egg yolk mixture in four batches, including all but 2 tablespoons of the double cream at the same time. Pour into the tin and place in the refrigerator until set.

9 Remove the sides of the tin, then, using a fish slice, carefully lift and slide the pudding onto a cold plate. Decorate with the remaining double cream and crystallized lemon slices.

Illustrated opposite page 160

Blackcurrant and Mint Mousse

SERVES 6

A pudding that speaks loudly of summer. Blackcurrants have a wonderful, intense, fresh-fruity flavour. Even if you do not have a garden, mints are one of the easiest herbs to grow, in pots if necessary, and it is worth having a selection of different flavoured mints, such as applemint and spearmint, as each has its own variation of the basic mint flavour. For this recipe, I chose applemint, because it combines so well with blackcurrants.

- 450 G/1 LB BLACKCURRANTS
- JUICE OF 1 LEMON
- 85 G/3 OZ CASTER SUGAR
- LEAVES FROM A SMALL BUNCH OF APPLEMINT
- 2 TBSP WATER
- 1 TBSP POWDERED GELATINE
- 2 EGG WHITES, SIZE 2
- 300 ML/10 FL OZ DOUBLE CREAM, WHIPPED
- 150 ML/5 FL OZ STRAINED GREEK YOGURT
- **DECORATION:**
- WHIPPED CREAM AND MINT LEAVES

1 Gently cook the blackcurrants in a covered saucepan, shaking the pan occasionally, until the juices run. Leave to cool slightly, then pour the fruit and all the juice into a food processor or blender and add the lemon juice, sugar and mint. Mix until smooth. Pour into a bowl.

2 Put the water into a small heatproof bowl, sprinkle over the gelatine and leave for about 5 minutes to soften. Set the bowl over a saucepan of hot water, stirring occasionally, until the gelatine has dissolved. Remove the bowl from the saucepan and leave to cool slightly before stirring in a little of the blackcurrant mixture, then whisk this into the remaining blackcurrant mixture. Leave until just beginning to set.

3 In a clean, dry bowl, whisk the egg whites until stiff but not dry. Whisk the blackcurrant mixture and whisk together the cream and yogurt. Using a large metal spoon, gently fold the cream mixture into the blackcurrant mixture, followed by the egg whites. Spoon into glasses or a serving dish and leave in the refrigerator for 1–2 hours to set.

4 Decorate with whipped cream, if liked, and mint leaves.

RIGHT (from top to bottom): Blackcurrant and Mint Mousse; Traditional Manor House Trifle (see page 151); Summer Pudding in a Special Jacket (see page 170).

CREAM CHEESE CAKE WITH PINE NUTS AND RASPBERRY SAUCE

SERVES 8

The raspberry sauce provides a suitably elegant and fresh complement to this luxurious yet simple cake. The whole pudding is also extremely easy to make and can be made a day in advance, although the cake is better if kept in a cool room rather than in the refrigerator. If you do not have a sufficiently cool room and have to refrigerate the cake, be sure to cover it, place it on the lowest shelf of the refrigerator, and allow it to come to room temperature before serving.

- 55 G/2 OZ UNSALTED BUTTER, SOFTENED
- 200 G/7 OZ VANILLA CASTER SUGAR
- 2 TBSP ACACIA HONEY
- 450 G/1 LB CREAM CHEESE, SIEVED
- 5 EGGS, SEPARATED
- 115 ML/4 FL OZ SINGLE CREAM
- 55 G/2 OZ PLAIN FLOUR
- 115 G/4 OZ PINE NUTS, CHOPPED
- **RASPBERRY SAUCE:**
- VANILLA ICING SUGAR, FOR SIFTING
- 700 G/1 ½ LB FRESH OR FROZEN RASPBERRIES
- ICING SUGAR AND LEMON JUICE, TO TASTE

1 Set the oven to 160°C/325°F/Gas 3. Butter a 20–22.5 cm/8–9 inch springform cake tin or loose-based cake tin.

2 Beat the butter and half the sugar together until light and airy, then beat in the honey followed by the cream cheese and egg yolks and lastly the cream. Using a large metal spoon, gently fold in the flour.

3 In a clean, dry bowl, whisk the egg whites until soft peaks form, then gradually whisk in the remaining sugar, whisking well after each addition, until the mixture is stiff and shiny. Using the metal spoon, gently fold one quarter into the cheese mixture. Fold in the remaining egg whites in three batches, adding the nuts with the last batch. Turn into the cake tin and bake for about 1 hour.

4 Leave the cake to cool in the oven with the heat turned off to prevent the cake cracking as it cools.

5 To make the sauce, Sieve the raspberries through a non-metallic sieve and add icing sugar and lemon juice to taste. Chill lightly.

6 Sift icing sugar generously over the cake and serve with the sauce.

LEFT (from top to bottom): Chestnut Compote with Coffee Sauce (see page 138); Cream Cheese Cake with Pine Nuts and Raspberry Sauce; Tiramisu with Torrone (see page 172).

PASKHA

SERVES 8

Traditionally, Paskha is eaten by Russians at Easter and it is made in a wooden mould shaped rather like a truncated metronome; a clay flowerpot, even a sieve, lined with muslin can be used instead. It will be easier to serve if you use a knife that has been dipped in hot water. Paskha is usually served on its own, but I like to serve it with a sauce made from sieved raspberries, strawberries or loganberries, sweetened to taste.

Place weights on the saucer and leave to drain

- 55 G/2 OZ CANDIED PEEL, CHOPPED
- 55 G/2 OZ CANDIED FRUITS, CHOPPED
- 55 G/2 OZ SULTANAS
- 3 TBSP WHITE RUM
- 115 G/4 OZ UNSALTED BUTTER, CHOPPED
- 85 G/3 OZ CASTER SUGAR
- 2 EGG YOLKS, SIZE 2
- 55 G/2 OZ BLANCHED ALMONDS, TOASTED AND CHOPPED
- FINELY GRATED RIND AND JUICE OF 1 LEMON
- FINELY GRATED RIND OF 1 ORANGE
- 150 ML/5 FL OZ SOURED CREAM
- 700 G/1½ LB RICOTTA OR CURD CHEESE, SIEVED
- **DECORATION:**
- WHOLE, BLANCHED ALMONDS
- CRYSTALLIZED VIOLETS

1 Soak the peel, candied fruits and sultanas in the rum overnight.

2 Wring out a piece of muslin in cold water, then use to line a conical mould, sieve or thoroughly cleaned or new flowerpot or plastic pot.

3 Beat together the butter and sugar until light and fluffy. Beat in the egg yolks, then mix in the chopped almonds, lemon rind and juice, orange rind, rum-soaked peel, candied fruits and sultanas. Using a tablespoon, fold in the soured cream and sieved cheese.

4 Stand the mould or pot on a large saucer and fill with the cheese mixture. Place a small saucer on the cheese mixture and put a weight on it. Place in the refrigerator and leave for at least 12 hours or up to 3 days.

5 Turn out onto a cold plate and carefully remove the muslin. Decorate with almonds and crystallized violets. Serve cut into thin slices.

Illustrated opposite page 128

CHOCOLATE MOUSSE CAKE

SERVES 6–8

I have many recipes for chocolate cakes and I have chosen this one for this book on puddings because, unlike most, it has neither the filling nor the icing, which make more of a gâteau-type cake than a pudding. This one doesn't need embellishments and has a wonderful soft, moist centre that is like a fudgy chocolate mousse. A raspberry sauce, made by sieving fresh or thawed frozen raspberries and sweetened to taste, does go very well with it, though. The finely grated rind of 2 small oranges, or 1–2 tablespoons brandy, whisky or rum, or about 1½ tablespoons coffee granules, or about 3 tablespoons crème de menthe *or coffee liqueur can be added to flavour the cake.*

- COCOA POWDER, FOR SPRINKLING
- 175 G/6 OZ PLAIN CHOCOLATE, CHOPPED
- 175 G/6 OZ UNSALTED BUTTER, DICED
- 175 G/6 OZ CASTER SUGAR
- 5 EGGS, SIZE 2, SEPARATED
- FEW DROPS VANILLA ESSENCE
- 55 G/2 OZ PLAIN FLOUR
- 85 G/3 OZ GROUND HAZELNUTS OR WALNUTS

1 Set the oven to 180°C/350°F/Gas 4. Butter a 20 cm/8 inch round cake tin and sprinkle the inside with cocoa powder.

2 Place the chocolate in a heatproof mixing bowl placed over a saucepan of hot, but not boiling, water and leave until melted. Slowly stir in the butter until evenly combined, then remove the bowl from the heat and stir in half of the sugar. Allow to cool slightly, then gradually beat in the egg yolks and vanilla essence. Stir in the flour and ground hazelnuts or walnuts.

3 In a separate clean, dry bowl, whisk the egg whites until soft peaks form, then gradually whisk in the remaining sugar, whisking well after each addition, until the mixture is stiff and shiny. Using a large metal spoon, gently fold into the chocolate mixture in batches. Spoon into the cake tin and bake for about 40 minutes; the cake should be moist in the middle.

4 Leave the cake to cool in the tin for about 10 minutes before turning onto a wire rack to cool completely.

Honeycombe Mould

SERVES 4

A clean, fresh-tasting nursery pudding that, despite its simplicity, makes a wonderful, surprisingly special ending to a meal, especially in summer.

- 2 TBSP COLD WATER
- 15 G/½ OZ POWDERED GELATINE
- 2 EGGS, SIZE 2, SEPARATED
- 85 G/3 OZ CASTER SUGAR
- 425 ML/15 FL OZ CREAMY MILK
- 85 ML/3 FL OZ SINGLE CREAM
- FINELY GRATED RIND OF 1 SMALL LEMON
- 4 TBSP LEMON JUICE

1 Chill a 1.2 litre/2 pint jelly mould or 4 individual moulds.

2 Put the water into a small heatproof bowl, sprinkle over the gelatine and leave for about 5 minutes to soften. Place the bowl over a saucepan of hot water, stirring occasionally, until the gelatine has dissolved.

3 Meanwhile, beat the egg yolks and sugar together until thick and pale. Bring the milk and cream to the boil in a heavy-based saucepan, then stir into the egg yolk mixture. Return to the saucepan and heat very gently, stirring with a wooden spoon, until thickened. Remove from the heat and stir in the lemon rind and juice.

4 As soon as the gelatine has dissolved, remove the bowl from the heat. Stir a couple of spoonfuls of the hot lemon custard into the gelatine, then stir this mixture into the saucepan.

5 In a clean, dry bowl, whisk the egg whites until stiff but not dry. Using a large metal spoon, gently fold into the hot custard.

6 Rinse the mould or moulds with cold water, drain well, then pour in the custard. Leave in a cool place to set.

BANANA BUTTERSCOTCH SUNDAE

SERVES 4

An unashamedly childish creation that everybody loves.

- 2 RIPE BANANAS
- LEMON JUICE
- VANILLA DAIRY ICE CREAM
- APPROXIMATELY 4 TBSP CHOPPED PEANUTS OR WALNUTS
- GRATED PLAIN CHOCOLATE OR CHOCOLATE CHIPS (OPTIONAL)
- BRANDY SNAPS, CRUSHED (OPTIONAL)

- **BUTTERSCOTCH SAUCE:**
- 115 ML/4 FL OZ EVAPORATED MILK
- 55 G/2 OZ UNSALTED BUTTER
- 85 G/3 OZ DARK MUSCOVADO SUGAR
- 3 TBSP GOLDEN SYRUP
- 1 TBSP WATER
- SQUEEZE OF LEMON JUICE

1 To make the sauce, put the evaporated milk in a heatproof bowl. In a saucepan, gently heat together the butter, sugar and syrup until well blended, stir in the water and bring to the boil. After a few seconds, remove from the heat and gradually beat into the evaporated milk. Return to the heat and heat through gently to make a smooth sauce. Cool slightly, then add a squeeze of lemon juice.

2 Peel and slice the bananas and toss with lemon juice. Pile scoops of vanilla dairy ice cream and slices of banana into glasses, sprinkling with as many nuts, and chocolate and brandy snaps, if liked, as you want. Pour the sauce over the top and sprinkle with more nuts, and brandy snaps and chocolate, if liked. Eat immediately.

Illustrated opposite page 129

SENSUOUS, SILKY SAFFRON CREAMS

SERVES 4

I can still remember the heady, exotic perfume that wafted sensuously from a 1 kg/2 lb tin of saffron as it was opened in front of me, even though it happened about seven years ago. It was far superior to any perfume man has produced, no matter how expensive. Saffron is costly, but the flavour and aroma are so intense that only a small amount is needed for 4–6 people, so the cost is not too high. Do not be tempted to buy a product that purports to be saffron if it seems cheap, as counterfeits are far too common; saffron threads are less likely to be adulterated than powders.

- SCANT ¼ TSP SAFFRON THREADS
- 4 EGG YOLKS
- 55 G/2 OZ LIGHT-FLAVOURED CLEAR HONEY
- 425 ML/15 FL OZ SINGLE CREAM

1 Set the oven to 140°C/275°F/Gas 1. Place 4 ramekin dishes or heatproof moulds in a baking tin.

2 Heat the saffron threads in a dry frying pan for 2–3 minutes, then crush them and put them into a medium-sized bowl and stir in the egg yolks and honey.

3 Heat the cream to just on simmering point, then stir into the egg yolk mixture. Return to the saucepan and heat very gently, stirring with a wooden spoon until thickened; do not allow to boil.

4 Pour into the ramekin dishes or moulds, pour boiling water around and place in the oven for 45 minutes to 1 hour until just set.

5 Remove the dishes or moulds from the baking tin and serve warm or cold.

TRADITIONAL MANOR HOUSE TRIFLE

SERVES 6 – 8

Warning: with a syllabub on a blanket of custard laid over wine and brandy-soaked fresh fruit and macaroons, this is one of the most luxurious trifles there is and makes an ideal ending to a special meal. Instead of using 5 egg yolks for the custard, you could use 2 egg yolks and 2 whole eggs.

- 6 LARGE MACAROONS
- 350 G/12 OZ PREPARED FRESH FRUIT, SUCH AS STRAWBERRIES, RASPBERRIES, PEACHES AND NECTARINES
- 150 ML/5 FL OZ DESSERT WINE SUCH AS BEAUMES-DE-VENISE
- 3½ TBSP BRANDY
- 425 ML/15 FL OZ SINGLE CREAM OR MILK
- 1 VANILLA POD
- 5 EGG YOLKS, SIZE 2
- 70 G/2½ OZ CASTER SUGAR
- FINELY GRATED RIND AND JUICE OF 1 LEMON
- 300 ML/10 FL OZ DOUBLE CREAM
- **DECORATION:**
- TOASTED FLAKED ALMONDS AND CRYSTALLIZED FRUITS

1 Put the macaroons into the base of a glass serving dish, cover with the fruit, then pour over 4 tablespoons of the wine and 2 tablespoons of brandy and leave to soak.

2 Make a custard (see page 181) with the cream or milk, vanilla pod, egg yolks and 2 tablespoons of the sugar. Allow to cool slightly, stirring occasionally, then pour over the fruit and leave to cool completely.

3 In a bowl, stir together the remaining wine, brandy and sugar and the lemon rind and juice until the sugar has dissolved. Gradually stir in the cream, then whisk until the cream holds its shape.

4 Spoon onto the custard and decorate with flaked almonds and crystallized fruits.

Illustrated opposite page 144

EASY CHOCOLATE MOUSSE

SERVES 4–6

I have been making this recipe for almost thirty years and although I have tasted innumerable other easy chocolate mousses, none scores more highly than this one: the ingredients are few and straightforward, it is easy and quick to make, and, most important of all, it is delicious to eat, with a deep, intense chocolate flavour, which a little coffee can enhance, and not at all sweet. If you really want to go to town, add a couple of tablespoons of brandy or a coffee or orange liqueur when stirring in the egg yolks and vanilla essence.

- 225 G/8 OZ GOOD PLAIN CHOCOLATE, CHOPPED
- 25 G/1 OZ UNSALTED BUTTER
- 1–2 TSP INSTANT COFFEE GRANULES (OPTIONAL)
- 4 EGGS, SEPARATED
- FEW DROPS VANILLA ESSENCE

1 Place the chocolate, butter and coffee, if using, in a heatproof bowl and place over a saucepan of hot water. Leave to melt, stirring occasionally, until smooth.

2 Remove the bowl from the pan and stir in the egg yolks and vanilla essence.

3 In a clean, dry bowl, whisk the egg whites until stiff but not dry. Using a large metal spoon, gently fold a quarter of the egg whites into the chocolate, then add the remaining egg whites in three batches. When just evenly combined, spoon into cold serving dishes. Place in the refrigerator for 30 to 60 minutes.

TANGY LIME SPONGE AND PARFAIT

SERVES 4–6

This is a moist, tangy, fragrant, cake-type pudding. For special occasions, I decorate the parfait with glazed lime rind (for method, see page 62) and serve the pudding with poached lime segments (for method, see page 124).

- 2 SMALL LIMES
- 3 EGGS
- 150 G/5 OZ CASTER SUGAR
- SEEDS FROM 10 CARDAMOM PODS, LIGHTLY TOASTED AND FINELY CRUSHED
- 55 G/2 OZ UNSALTED BUTTER, MELTED AND COOLED
- 125 G/4½ OZ PLAIN FLOUR
- 1 TSP BAKING POWDER
- **LIME PARFAIT:**
- 2 EGG WHITES, SIZE 2
- 115 G/4 OZ CASTER SUGAR
- 4½ TBSP LIME JUICE
- 175 ML/6 FL OZ DOUBLE OR WHIPPING CREAM, LIGHTLY WHIPPED

1 To make the parfait, in a bowl, whisk the egg whites until soft peaks form. In a small saucepan, gently heat the sugar in the lime juice until dissolved. Increase the heat, bring to the boil and boil for 3 minutes. Slowly pour the mixture into the egg whites, whisking constantly. Using a large metal spoon, gently fold in the cream. Transfer to a shallow metal container and freeze for 3 hours. Transfer to the refrigerator about 20 minutes before serving.

2 Set the oven to just below 180°C/350°F/Gas 4. Well-butter a 15 cm/6 inch soufflé dish.

3 Peel the limes. Chop the pith and skin and simmer, just covered by water, in a small covered saucepan for about 35 minutes until tender. Increase the heat towards the end of the cooking time to evaporate off excess water.

4 Meanwhile, in a bowl placed over a saucepan of hot water, whisk the eggs and sugar together until very thick.

5 In a blender or food processor, purée the lime flesh with the cardamom seeds, then mix in the peel and pith and the butter. Slowly pour into the egg mixture, folding in gently with a large metal spoon. Sift the flour and baking powder over the top, then fold in lightly, using the metal spoon.

6 As soon as the ingredients are just evenly mixed, turn into the dish and bake for about 35–40 minutes, until a skewer inserted in the centre comes out clean.

7 Turn onto a wire rack to cool. Serve with scoops of parfait.

CHOCOLATE AND MINT ICE CREAM CAKE

SERVES 6–8

My birthday is in July and when I was young my birthday cake was always an ice cream one, and ever since I have had a soft spot for ice cream cakes. For me, an ice cream cake should include a proper cake, not just layers of different-flavoured ice creams, as there is something magical about the combination of cake and ice cream. This is one of my favourites, as it is suitable for any time of year and appeals to a wide range of tastes.

- **CHOCOLATE CAKE:**
- 200 G/7 OZ DARK SWEETENED CHOCOLATE, CHOPPED
- 5 TBSP WATER
- 5 EGGS, SEPARATED
- 150 G/5 OZ VANILLA CASTER SUGAR
- **PEPPERMINT ICE CREAM:**
- 175 G/6 OZ CASTER SUGAR
- 300 ML/10 FL OZ WATER
- JUICE OF 1 LEMON
- 2 TBSP FINELY CHOPPED MINT, PREFERABLY PEPPERMINT
- APPROXIMATELY 6 DROPS PEPPERMINT ESSENCE
- 425 ML/15 FL OZ DOUBLE CREAM, WHIPPED
- 100 G/3½ OZ PLAIN CHOCOLATE CHIPS
- **CHOCOLATE ICING:**
- 175 G/6 OZ PLAIN CHOCOLATE, CHOPPED
- 25 G/1 OZ UNSALTED BUTTER
- 1 TBSP WATER
- **DECORATION:**
- WHIPPED CREAM (OPTIONAL)
- FRESH MINT SPRIGS (OPTIONAL)
- **TO SERVE:**
- CHOCOLATE MINT SAUCE (SEE PAGE 184)

1 To make the peppermint ice cream, gently heat the sugar in the water in a heavy-based saucepan, stirring with a wooden spoon, until the sugar has dissolved, then bring to the boil and boil rapidly for a couple of minutes. Leave to cool, then pour into a shallow metal container and freeze for about 1½ hours until mushy. Tip into a cold bowl and fold in the lemon juice, mint leaves, peppermint essence, cream and chocolate chips. Taste and adjust the level of peppermint, if necessary. Spoon into a freezer-proof container, cover and freeze.

2 To make the chocolate cake, set the oven to 180°C/350°F/Gas 4. Butter two 20 cm/8 inch sandwich tins, line the base of each with greaseproof paper, then butter the paper.

3 Put the chocolate and the water into a heatproof bowl placed over a saucepan of hot water. Leave to melt, stirring occasionally, until smooth. Remove the bowl from the pan and leave the chocolate to cool slightly.

4 Meanwhile, in a separate bowl, whisk the egg yolks and half of the sugar together until very thick and pale.

5 In a clean, dry bowl, whisk the egg whites until soft peaks form, then gradually whisk in the remaining sugar, whisking well after each addition, until the mixture is stiff and shiny. Using a large metal spoon, gently fold the chocolate into the egg yolk mixture, then fold in the egg whites in four batches. Divide between the cake tins and bake for about 15–18 minutes until springy to a light touch in the centre.

6 Allow to stand for a few minutes (do not worry if they sink slightly), then turn onto a wire rack and carefully peel off the lining.

7 To assemble the cake, leave the ice cream at room temperature for about 20 minutes to soften slightly while making the icing. Put the chocolate and butter for the icing with the water into a heatproof bowl placed over a saucepan of hot water and leave to melt, stirring occasionally. Spread the ice cream over one of the chocolate cakes, then place the other cake on top and press lightly together. Quickly spread the icing over the top and sides and return to the freezer for 30 minutes to 1 hour. Decorate the top of the cake with spoonfuls of whipped cream placed in a circle with a sprig of mint in each, if liked, and serve the cake in slices with the Chocolate Mint Sauce poured over or around.

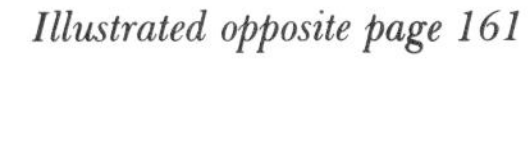

Illustrated opposite page 161

ROSE OR DAMASK CREAMS

SERVES 4

Yet another name for this old-fashioned pudding is 'Devonshire junket', but I feared some people might not look at the recipe if it bore that title. This light, delicate, subtly-flavoured dessert makes a perfect ending to a summer meal, or a heavy one, and I urge anyone who is doubtful to try it. Chemists as well as food shops sometime sell rennet essence; on no account use junket mix.

- 550 ML/1 PINT SINGLE CREAM
- 3 TBSP CASTER SUGAR
- 2 TSP RENNET ESSENCE
- 1 TBSP BRANDY
- 4 TBSP DOUBLE CREAM
- 1–2 TSP ROSE WATER
- **DECORATION:**
- ROSE PETALS (OPTIONAL)

1 Very gently heat the cream with 2 tablespoons of the sugar, stirring to dissolve the sugar, until the temperature reaches 36.9°C/98.4°F, or it feels neither hot nor cold when tested by dipping in a clean finger.

2 Stir in the rennet and brandy, then pour into a serving dish. Leave, undisturbed, for 2–3 hours until set.

3 Stir together the remaining sugar, the double cream and rose water to taste. Carefully spoon over the top of the set junket and decorate with rose petals, if liked.

CRUNCHY OATEN HIGHLAND CREAM WITH BERRIES

SERVES 4

I always associate this type of pudding, the ingredients layered in a tall glass, with childhood treats, but I cannot remember ever being given one quite like this when I was a child.

- 55 G/2 OZ UNSALTED BUTTER
- 55 G/2 OZ LIGHT MUSCOVADO SUGAR
- 55 G/2 OZ WALNUT HALVES, CHOPPED
- 25 G/1 OZ JUMBO OATS, TOASTED AND COOLED
- 4 TBSP WHISKY
- 300 ML/10 FL OZ DOUBLE CREAM, WHIPPED
- 350 G/12 OZ FRESH RASPBERRIES OR BLACKBERRIES
- **TO SERVE:**
- LIGHTLY WHIPPED DOUBLE CREAM (OPTIONAL)

1 Oil a baking sheet.

2 Melt the butter, stir in the sugar and heat gently, stirring with a wooden spoon, until the sugar has melted. Stir in the walnuts and oats, and cook until a light golden colour. Tip onto the baking sheet, leave until cold, then roughly crush.

3 Lightly fold the nut mixture and whisky into the cream using a large metal spoon.

4 Reserve a few of the berries for decoration and layer the remainder with the cream mixture in goblets or tall glasses. Cover and chill. Return to room temperture about 30 minutes before serving. Top with extra double cream, if liked. Decorate with the reserved berries.

BROWN SUGAR MERINGUES WITH EGG NOG PARFAIT AND ORANGE COMPOTE

SERVES 4–6

Brown sugar gives the meringues a caramel taste, which takes the edge off their sweetness and forms a very good partnership with the fresh taste of the orange compote and the smooth texture of the parfait. The meringues could more simply be sandwiched together with whipped cream flavoured with Cointreau.

- 4 ORANGES
- APPROXIMATELY 5 MM/¼ IN SLICE FRESH ROOT GINGER, PEELED AND CUT INTO FINE STRIPS
- 2 TBSP WHISKY LIQUEUR
- 115 G/4 OZ CASTER SUGAR
- 150 ML/5 FL OZ WATER
- JUICE OF ½ LEMON
- **EGG NOG PARFAIT:**
- 2 EGG YOLKS, SIZE 3
- 70 G/2½ OZ CASTER SUGAR
- ¼–½ TSP FRESHLY GRATED NUTMEG
- VERY SMALL PINCH OF GROUND CLOVES
- 55 ML/2 FL OZ PALE CREAM SHERRY
- 300 ML/10 FL OZ DOUBLE CREAM, LIGHTLY WHIPPED
- **MERINGUES:**
- 2 EGG WHITES, SIZE 3
- 85 G/3 OZ LIGHT MUSCOVADO SUGAR
- 25 G/1 OZ CASTER SUGAR

1 To make the egg nog parfait, whisk together the egg yolks, sugar, spices and sherry in a medium-sized heatproof bowl placed over a saucepan of hot water until pale and thick enough to support a trail of mixture when the beaters are withdrawn. Remove from the heat and continue to whisk until the mixture is cold. Using a large metal spoon, gently fold in the cream. Spoon into a shallow freezer-proof container, cover, chill, then freeze until firm.

2 To make the compote, cut a slice from each end of each orange then stand one fruit upright on a flat plate, to catch any juice. Then, using a flexible, sharp knife and working around the orange, cut down to remove both the peel and the pith. Repeat with the remaining oranges. Slice the oranges crosswise and put the slices in a serving bowl with any orange juice collected on the plate, the ginger and liqueur.

3 Scrape the pith from the orange peel, then cut the peel into strips. Put the strips into a small saucepan, cover well with water and bring to the boil for a couple of minutes. Drain and repeat the process; this will remove some of the bitterness from the peel. Cover with water again and simmer for 25–30 minutes until just tender. Drain the peel.

4 In a small saucepan, dissolve the sugar in the water. Add the strips of orange peel and simmer for 2–3 minutes until the peel begins to look glazed and candied. Add the lemon juice then pour the strips and syrup over the orange slices. Cover and place in the refrigerator for several hours.

5 To make the meringues, set the oven to 110°C/225°F/Gas ½. Line 1 or 2 baking trays, depending on size, with non-stick baking parchment, or greaseproof paper and brush lightly with flavourless vegetable oil.

6 In a clean, dry bowl, whisk the egg whites until stiff but not dry, then gradually whisk in the sugars, whisking well after each addition, until the mixture is stiff and shiny.

7 Place dessertspoonfuls of the meringue a little distance away from each other on the baking trays and bake for about 2 hours until crisp and dry enough to remove easily from the paper. Carefully remove from the paper and place the meringues on a wire rack.

8 Transfer the egg nog parfait to the refrigerator about 30 minutes before serving. Sandwich the meringues with some of the parfait then serve with the compote. Any remaining parfait can be served separately, or eaten on some other occasion.

Illustrated opposite page 129

SNOW EGGS ON A CARAMEL LAKE

SERVES 4

These meringue 'snowballs' are usually floated on a plain vanilla custard, but I think the addition of caramel makes a more interesting combination, which the threads of bitter caramel on top further enhance.

Float spoonfuls of the meringue on the milk

- 2 WHOLE EGGS, SIZE 2, SEPARATED
- 55 G/2 OZ VANILLA CASTER SUGAR
- 450 ML/6 FL OZ MILK OR A MIXTURE OF MILK AND CREAM
- 115 G/4 OZ CASTER OR GRANULATED SUGAR
- 3 EGG YOLKS, SIZE 2
- **CARAMEL:**
- 55 G/2 OZ CASTER OR GRANULATED SUGAR

1 In a clean, dry bowl, whisk the egg whites until soft peaks form, then gradually whisk in the vanilla caster sugar, whisking well after each addition, until the mixture is stiff and shiny.

2 Gently heat the milk to simmering point, then, taking care not to crowd them, float teaspoonfuls or small tablespoonfuls of the meringue, depending on the size you want the 'islands', on the milk. Poach for about 30 seconds to 1 minute on each side. Lift out using a slotted spoon and leave on a tea towel or wire rack to drain. Repeat until all the meringue has been cooked.

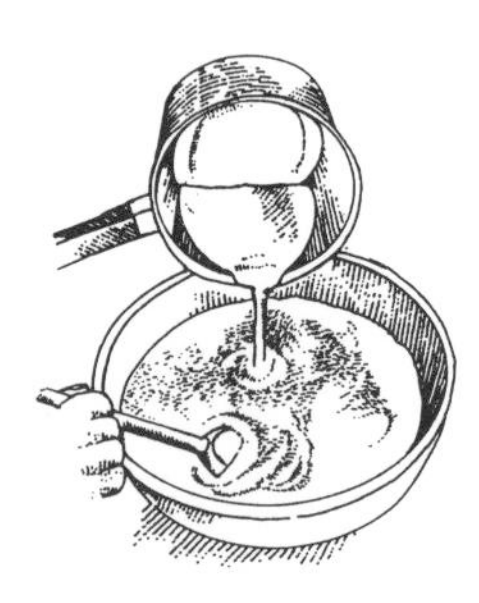

Slowly pour the milk into the egg yolks, stirring constantly

3 In a heavy-based saucepan, gently heat the caster or granulated sugar, stirring with a wooden spoon, until the sugar dissolves to a rich golden caramel. Remove from the heat and immediately slowly pour in the milk – take care as it will spit at first. Return the saucepan to a low heat and stir until the caramel dissolves. Remove from the heat.

4 Whisk together all the egg yolks until thick, then slowly stir in the caramel-flavoured milk. Return to the saucepan and heat gently, stirring constantly, until thickened; do not allow to boil. Remove from the heat, pour into a bowl and leave to cool to lukewarm, stirring occasionally to prevent a skin forming. Pour the custard into a shallow serving dish and leave until cold. Float the meringues on top of the custard.

5 To make the caramel, gently heat the sugar until dissolved, then cook until golden brown. Remove from the heat and immediately trickle over the islands; if liked, a little of the caramel can be used to spin a 'veil' over the finished pudding.

RIGHT (from top to bottom): Snow Eggs on a Caramel Lake; Voluptuous Chestnut, Chocolate and Rum Cake (see page 174); Forgotten Lemon Heaven (see page 142).

TANGERINE SYLLABUB

SERVES 4

That syllabubs were made by milking a cow into a bowl of spiced ale or wine is fairly often mentioned, but the origins of the word 'syllabub', which I think is an unusual one, remain ignored. The only explanation I have found so far is that it comes from the old French for Champagne, sille, *and the Elizabethan slang for a bubbling drink, bub;* sille *was mixed with frothy cream to make a 'sille bub'! It sounds plausible, if rather contrived. No matter how it got its name, this is my favourite syllabub.*

- 700 G/1½ LB TANGERINES (ABOUT 6)
- 2 TBSP LEMON JUICE
- 2 TBSP COINTREAU OR OTHER ORANGE LIQUEUR
- 55 G/2 OZ LIGHT MUSCOVADO SUGAR
- 300 ML/10 FL OZ DOUBLE CREAM
- **DECORATION:**
- TANGERINE ZEST, CUT INTO JULIENNE (OPTIONAL)

1 Finely grate the rind from three tangerines into a small bowl; use a stiff brush to remove all the rind from the teeth of the grater. Peel these three tangerines, divide into segments, then carefully remove and discard the skin surrounding each segment. Cover and place in the refrigerator to use for decorating the syllabub.

2 Halve and squeeze the remaining tangerines and pour the juice over the grated rind. Add the lemon juice and liqueur, then cover and leave for at least 2 hours in a cool place or in the refrigerator.

3 Stir the sugar into the fruit juices until dissolved, then stir in the cream and whip until stiff. Spoon into glasses or individual glass dishes and chill for at least 2 hours. Serve decorated with the tangerine segments, and tangerine zest cut into julienne.

Illustrated opposite page 128

LEFT (from top to bottom): Christmas Pudding (see page 66); Chocolate and Mint Ice Cream Cake (see page 154); Succulent, Smooth Apple Cake (see page 36), served with Fluffy Orange Sauce (see page 184).

CHEESECAKE

SERVES 8

After I had recovered from the initial shock of discovering that cheesecake was not savoury, when I first went to France in the late Fifties, I have loved cheesecake. As soon as I see a recipe, I scrutinize it minutely. I tend to favour traditional French-style baked versions, although I do prefer biscuit-crumb bases to pastry, providing they are not too sweet or too much in evidence. This recipe is one of the simplest I have among my vast collection, and one of the ones I most enjoy. The mixture appears to be a little soft in the centre at the end of the stated one hour's cooking time, but it firms up as it cools.

- 20 G/¾ OZ UNSALTED BUTTER
- 85 G/3 OZ DIGESTIVE BISCUITS, FINELY CRUSHED
- 550 G/1¼ LB GOOD CREAM CHEESE, SIEVED
- 150 ML/5 FL OZ SOURED CREAM
- 175 G/6 OZ CASTER SUGAR
- 4 EGGS, SIZE 3, SEPARATED
- GRATED RIND OF 2 ORANGES

- **ORANGE SAUCE (OPTIONAL):**
- 3 LARGE ORANGES
- APPROXIMATELY 150 G/5 OZ CASTER SUGAR
- 2 TBSP WATER
- JUICE OF ½ LEMON
- **TO FINISH:**
- ICING SUGAR, GROUND CINNAMON AND FRESHLY GRATED NUTMEG, FOR SIFTING

1 Set the oven to 160°C/325°F/Gas 3. Line the base and sides of a 25 cm/10 inch loose-based or springform cake tin with greaseproof paper.

2 In a small saucepan, gently melt the butter. Remove from the heat and stir in the crushed biscuits. Transfer to the cake tin and press firmly into the base and sides to make an even shell.

3 In a large bowl, beat the cream cheese until smooth, then gradually beat in the soured cream followed by the sugar, egg yolks and orange rind.

4 In a separate, clean, dry bowl, whisk the egg whites until stiff but not dry. Using a large metal spoon, gently fold into the cheese mixture. Spoon into the cake tin and level the surface. Bake for 1 hour. Leave to cool in the tin.

5 To make the sauce, thinly pare the rind from the oranges, taking care not to include any white pith. Cut the rind into fine strips and place in a small saucepan with enough cold water to cover. Bring to the boil, then simmer until soft and slightly transparent. Tip into a non-metallic sieve to drain. In the same saucepan, gently heat the sugar in the water, stirring with a wooden spoon, until dissolved, then stir in the lemon juice, the juice of the oranges and the strips of rind. Simmer for 2 minutes, then pour into a small jug or sauceboat. Leave to cool, then chill lightly.

6 Liberally sift a mixture of icing sugar, cinnamon and ground nutmeg over the cheesecake and serve with the sauce, if liked.

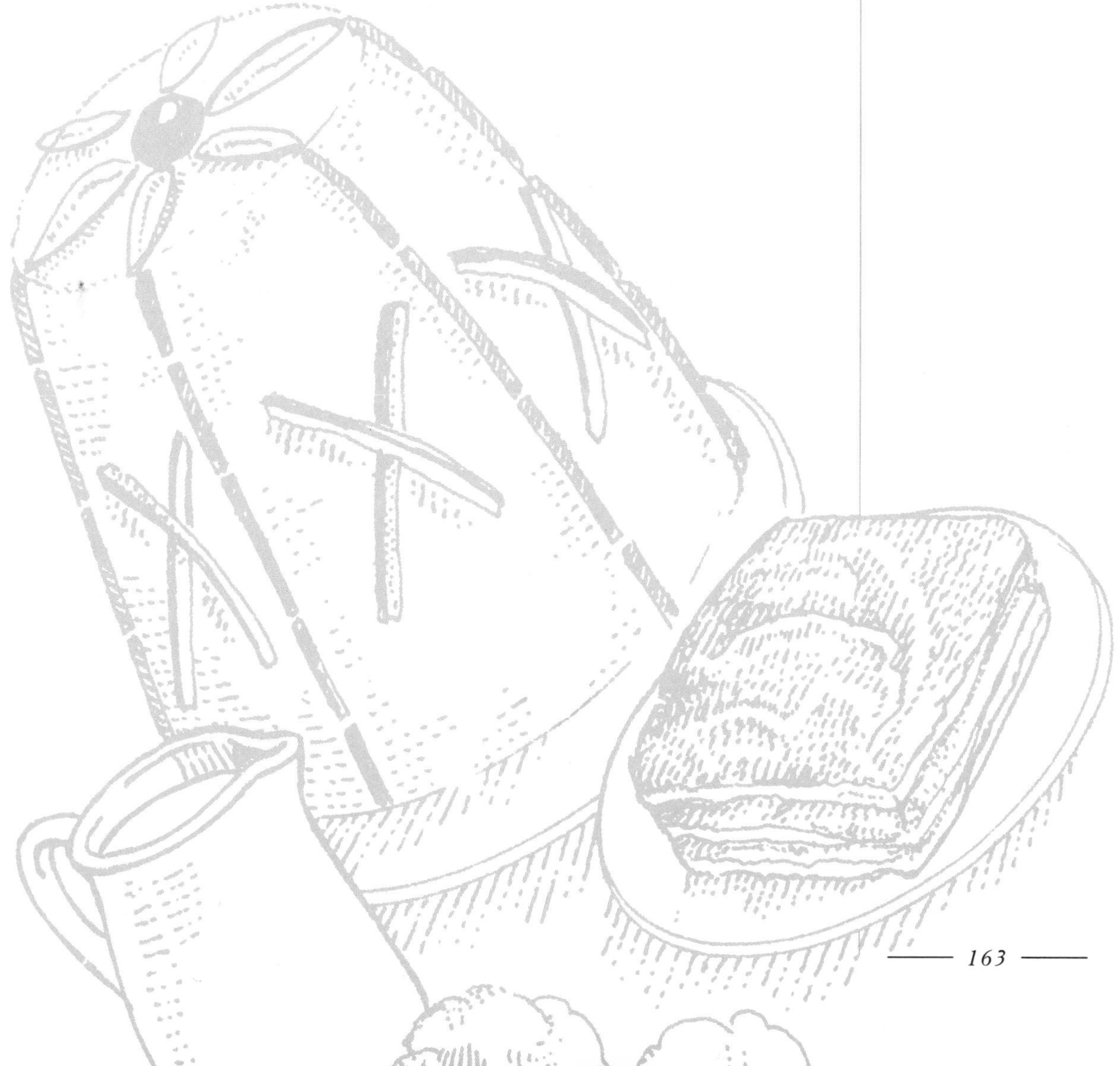

GOOSEBERRY FOOL

SERVES 4

Fools are one of our oldest puddings. They date back to the sixteenth and seventeenth centuries and belong to the same family as trifles and whim whams. Fools sometimes combine just fruit and whipped cream, but for a gooseberry fool, which is one of my favourites and one of the least often seen, I prefer to make a creamy custard, as I think the flavour and texture combination is superior; the consistency is softer and the flavour fresher. In early summer, try to get a head of elderflowers (but not from roadside bushes) to add to the gooseberries – they add a magical muscat flavour.

- 550 G/1 ¼ LB GOOSEBERRIES, TOPPED AND TAILED
- 4 TBSP DRY WHITE WINE OR WATER
- 2 EGG YOLKS, SIZE 3
- 25 G/1 OZ CASTER SUGAR, PLUS EXTRA TO TASTE
- 150 ML/5 FL OZ MILK
- 150 ML/5 FL OZ DOUBLE CREAM, WHIPPED
- ORANGE FLOWER WATER (OPTIONAL)

1 Gently cook the gooseberries in the wine or water in a covered saucepan until just tender, shaking the pan occasionally. Leave to cool in the liquid, then crush with a fork in the cooking juices; if you prefer a smooth fool, purée both the fruit and the cooking juices, then pass through a non-metallic sieve.

2 Meanwhile, whisk together the egg yolks and 25 g/1 oz sugar in a small, heatproof bowl. Bring the milk to the boil, then slowly stir into the egg mixture. Place the bowl over a saucepan of hot water and cook, stirring with a wooden spoon, until thickened. Remove the bowl from the heat and allow the mixture to cool, stirring occasionally to prevent a skin forming.

3 Gently stir the cooled custard into the gooseberries, then gently fold in the double cream, using a large metal spoon. Add sugar to taste and flavour with orange flower water, if liked. Spoon into 4 tall glasses, cover and chill lightly.

ITALIAN COFFEE CREAM AND WALNUT CAKE

SERVES 6–8

The perennially popular partnership between coffee and walnut is particularly enjoyable in this recipe, as the cake is light and nutty with a delicate crumb, and the filling and topping rich and deeply flavoured with coffee.

- 3 EGGS, SIZE 2, SEPARATED
- 115 G/4 OZ LIGHT MUSCOVADO SUGAR
- 25 G/1 OZ UNSALTED BUTTER, MELTED AND COOLED
- 125 G/4½ OZ WALNUT HALVES, GROUND
- 1 TBSP STRONG COFFEE, PREFERABLY ESPRESSO
- 1 TBSP FINE BREADCRUMBS

FILLING AND TOPPING

- 1 EGG, SIZE 2, SEPARATED
- 25–55 G/1–2 OZ SUGAR
- 250 G/9 OZ MASCARPONE CHEESE
- 1½–2 TBSP STRONG COFFEE, PREFERABLY ESPRESSO
- FEW DROPS VANILLA ESSENCE

DECORATION:

- COFFEE BEANS AND WALNUT HALVES

1 Set the oven to 180°C/350°F/Gas 4. Butter a 17.5 cm/7 inch springform, non-stick cake tin.

2 Whisk the egg yolks and half the sugar together until thick and light. Using a large metal spoon, fold in the butter, walnuts, coffee and breadcrumbs.

3 In a clean, dry bowl, whisk the egg whites until soft peaks form, then gradually whisk in the remaining sugar until stiff. Using a metal spoon, very gently fold into the walnut mixture. Spoon into the tin and bake for about 35 minutes until a fine skewer inserted in the centre comes out clean.

4 Leave to cool in the tin for a few minutes before turning onto a wire rack.

5 To make the filling and topping, whisk the egg yolk with the sugar in a medium-sized bowl until thick and light. Using a large metal spoon, fold in the mascarpone a tablespoonful at a time, then add the coffee and vanilla essence. In a clean, dry bowl, whisk the egg white until stiff, then, using the metal spoon, gently fold into the mascarpone mixture. Cover and place in the refrigerator.

6 About 2 hours before serving the cake, cut in half horizontally using a bread knife and spread about a quarter of the mascarpone mixture over the bottom half. Replace the top and spread the remaining mascarpone mixture over the top and sides. Decorate with coffee beans and walnut halves and keep in a cool place until required.

Illustrated opposite page 129

TRADITIONAL WHITE BLANCMANGE WITH RED BERRIES

SERVES 4–6

The earliest known blancmanges were made in medieval times: a mixture of cooked white meats, such as pork and chicken, or white fish on Fridays, pounded to a pulp, then combined with almond milk, boiled rice and sugar. By the reign of Elizabeth I, meatless versions existed, using cream, rose water and sugar and eggs for thickening. In the seventeenth and eighteenth centuries, isinglass was used to set the blancmange; and arrowroot, the precursor of cornflour, was introduced as a thickener in the nineteenth century after it was imported from the West Indies. In this century food companies such as Brown and Polson took blancmange over and I should think the number of people who made blancmange from scratch rather than use a packet could be counted on one hand. I used to love butterscotch blancmange – hot and in quantity. This flavour is no longer made because, to quote, 'there is no demand'. It is impossible to replicate the taste of the butterscotch flavouring used, so I now make a very different type of blancmange – one that makes a very special end to a summer meal.

- 115 G/4 OZ BLANCHED ALMONDS, GROUND
- 450 ML/16 FL OZ MILK
- 4 TSP CORNFLOUR
- APPROXIMATELY 3 TBSP CASTER SUGAR
- 150 ML/5 FL OZ WHIPPING CREAM, WHIPPED
- APPROXIMATELY 1½ TSP ORANGE FLOWER WATER
- 375 G/13 OZ RIPE STRAWBERRIES
- 100 ML/3½ FL OZ DESSERT WINE
- ABOUT 2 TBSP ORANGE JUICE
- 250 G/9 OZ RASPBERRIES
- 1–2 TBSP FRAMBOISE LIQUEUR

1 Rinse a decorative 550 ml/1 pint ring mould with cold water, then leave upside down to drain. Line a sieve with muslin.

2 Gently heat the ground almonds and the milk to simmering point, cover and leave in a warm place for 15 minutes. Pour the mixture into a blender or food processor and process for several seconds. Pour through the sieve, pressing down well to extract all the milk.

3 In a small bowl, mix together 2 tablespoons of the milk, the cornflour and sugar. In a saucepan, bring the remaining milk to the boil, stir a little into the bowl, then pour back into the saucepan and return to the boil, stirring with a wooden spoon. Cook gently for about 3 minutes.

4 Allow the mixture to cool slightly, then, using a large metal spoon, gently fold in the cream and flavour judicially with orange flower water. Pour into the mould and leave for several hours to set.

5 Reserve about 150 g/5 oz of the strawberries. Slice or quarter the remaining strawberries, according to size, place in a bowl and pour over the wine and orange juice. Leave in a cold place for 1–2 hours.

6 To serve the pudding, dampen the centre of a cold plate, place it over the mould, then, holding the two together, invert them and give a sharp shake. Carefully lift off the mould. Drain and reserve the juices from the strawberries. Mix the berries with about 175 g/6 oz of the raspberries and pile in the centre of the blancmange. Purée the juices with the framboise liqueur, reserved strawberries and remaining raspberries. Adjust the taste with orange juice or sugar, if necessary, then trickle some over the blancmange, some over the fruit and serve the rest separately.

ORANGE-FLAVOURED BABAS WITH KUMQUATS

SERVES 6

With easy-blend yeasts, and food processors and mixers, cooking with yeast has become so simple, especially when you realize that the dough does not have to be left for a specific time in a warm place to rise. It will in fact rise at room temperature, even in the refrigerator – the only difference is that it will take longer. You can, therefore, fit the rising in with your other arrangements by purposefully selecting the appropriate place in which to leave the dough.

BABAS:

- 200 G/7 OZ STRONG PLAIN FLOUR
- PINCH OF SALT
- 1 PACKET EASY-BLEND DRIED YEAST
- 125 ML/4½ FL OZ WARM MILK
- 2 EGGS SIZE 2, BEATEN
- 1 TBSP CLEAR HONEY
- 55 G/2 OZ UNSALTED BUTTER, SOFTENED

SYRUP AND FILLING:

- 225 G/8 OZ CLEAR HONEY
- 2.5 CM/1 IN CINNAMON STICK
- 225 ML/8 FL OZ WATER
- 6 TBSP DARK RUM
- 3 TBSP COINTREAU
- 250 G/9 OZ KUMQUATS

TO SERVE:

- 300 ML/10 FL OZ *CRÈME FRAÎCHE*

1 To make the syrup, in a medium-sized saucepan, gently heat the honey with the cinnamon in the water, stirring occasionally with a wooden spoon, until the honey has melted. Bring to the boil, simmer for a couple of minutes, then remove from the heat and stir in the rum and Cointreau.

2 Remove the cinnamon and pour off half the syrup and reserve. Poach the kumquats in the syrup remaining in the saucepan for about 15–20 minutes until tender, then leave to cool in the syrup.

3 To make the babas, sift the flour and salt into a bowl, stir in the yeast and form a well in the centre. Mix together the milk, eggs and honey, then slowly pour into the well in the flour, drawing the dry ingredients into the liquid using a wooden spoon, to make a smooth dough. With your hand, beat well until the dough becomes firm and elastic. Dot the butter over the surface, cover the bowl with a damp cloth or cling film and leave until doubled in volume – 45 minutes to 1 hour in a warm place, 1½ hours in a cool one.

4 Well butter six 9 cm/3½ inch ring moulds.

5 Turn the dough onto a lightly floured work surface and knead lightly. Divide into 6 equal portions and fit into the moulds. Cover loosely and leave until risen to the top of the moulds.

6 Set the oven to 200°C/400°F/Gas 6. Bake the babas for 10–15 minutes until risen and golden. Allow to cool slighty, then turn onto a wire rack for 5 minutes.

7 Using a slotted spoon, remove the kumquats from the syrup and slice thinly. Pour the reserved syrup back into the saucepan and heat gently without allowing it to boil.

8 Prick the babas all over with a fork, then return them to the ring moulds. Slowly spoon over the hot syrup and continue to spoon it over the babas until they are thoroughly saturated.

9 To serve, unmould the babas, place the sliced kumquats over and around. Serve with *crème fraîche* and any remaining syrup.

Illustrated opposite page 128

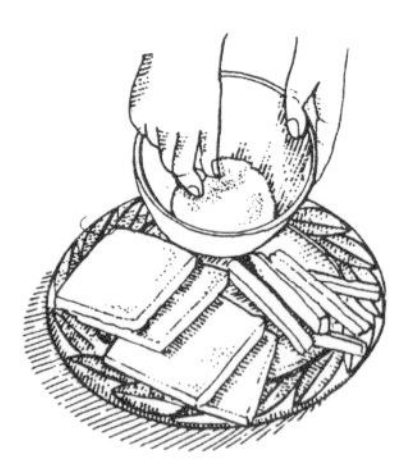

Place the circle of sponge in the bottom of the basin

Line the sides of the basin with sponge

Fill with fruit

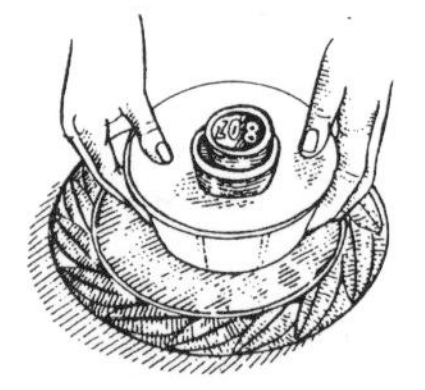

Cover with a plate or saucer; place weights on top

SUMMER PUDDING IN A SPECIAL JACKET

SERVES 6

I love fruit, but I had a long-standing aversion to traditional summer pudding and to its more recently popularized cousins, autumn and winter puddings. The first summer pudding I ate was in the late Fifties, and it had been made using sliced white bread. I found the texture of the bread so unacceptable that I steadfastly avoided the pudding for years. I was coaxed into trying it with a jacket of brioche – better, I admit, but I still preferred to have the fruit on its own. Then a friend said she used a sponge cake to line the basin. Eureka! At last, something that was a more suitable partner to the fruit, especially sun-ripened summer ones. For the freshest, most fruity flavour, use a gentle heat that will coax the juices from the fruit, and use the ripest fruit you can to minimize the heating they need; the juice of really ripe red fruits will run without any heating at all – just sprinkle them with sugar and leave until the juice runs naturally. The fruits can, of course, be varied according to personal taste and what is available.

- 225 G/8 OZ BLACKCURRANTS
- CASTER SUGAR
- 700 G/1 ½ LB MIXED RIPE RED SUMMER FRUITS, SUCH AS RASPBERRIES, STRAWBERRIES, REDCURRANTS, STONED CHERRIES
- 8–10 SLICES SPONGE CAKE, PREFERABLY HOME-MADE AND NOT TOO SWEET (SEE NOTE)
- **TO SERVE:**
- FRESH FRUIT AND *CRÈME FRAÎCHE*

1 In a saucepan, mix the blackcurrants with 2 or 3 tablespoons of sugar, leave for a short while, then cover and heat gently, shaking the pan occasionally, until the fruit juices begin to run. Add the red fruits and continue to heat gently until their juices run. Add a little more sugar, if necessary, but do not forget that the cake is slightly sweet and will sweeten the juices; I sometimes like to keep the fruit unsweetened so that it makes more of a contrast to the cake.

2 Cut a circle from 1 slice of cake to neatly fit the bottom of a 1.2 litre/2 pint pudding basin. Fit the circle into the basin, then line it with most of the remaining slices, overlapping them slightly and making sure there are no gaps. Spoon the fruit and most of the juices into the basin, taking care not to dislodge the cake lining; reserve about 3 tablespoons of the juice. Cover with the remaining cake. Cover the top of the basin with greaseproof paper, then with foil and place a saucer or small plate that just fits inside the bowl on top. Place a heavy weight on the saucer or plate. Put in the refrigerator overnight.

3 To serve, run the point of a sharp knife carefully around the edge of the pudding, then invert the pudding onto a serving plate. Spoon the reserved juices over the top and place fruit around the bottom. Serve with *crème fraîche*.

NOTE: Make a Swiss roll sponge in a Swiss roll tin.

Illustrated opposite page 144

TIRAMISU WITH TORRONE

SERVES 4–6

Tiramisu is a comparatively recent creation of the owner of the El Toula restaurant in Treviso, Italy, but it is served so often in restaurants (not just Italian ones), and so many recipes have been published for it, that many people believe it is a traditional pudding. Torrone 'nougat' is not a traditional ingredient in Tiramisu, but it does give it that extra je ne sais quoi, *providing a good, firm, chewy nougat is used. Italy and Spain both produce some excellent nougats. Christmas is a good time to look, particularly in Italian and Spanish speciality food shops, as the nougat is a popular Christmas treat. Chop the nougat using a food processor or blender.*

- 2 EGGS, SEPARATED
- 2 TBSP SOFT BROWN SUGAR
- 300 G/10 OZ MASCARPONE CHEESE
- 115 G/4 OZ TORRONE, FINELY CHOPPED
- 150 G/5 OZ PLAIN CHOCOLATE, FINELY CHOPPED (OPTIONAL)
- 150 ML/5 FL OZ FRESHLY MADE GOOD STRONG COFFEE, PREFERABLY ESPRESSO, COOLED
- 100 ML/3½ FL OZ COFFEE LIQUEUR SUCH AS TIA MARIA OR KAHLUA
- 18 ITALIAN SAVOIARDI SPONGE FINGERS OR GOOD-QUALITY ORDINARY SPONGE FINGERS
- COCOA POWDER (OPTIONAL)

1 Whisk together the egg yolks and sugar in a large bowl until thick and pale, then gradually whisk in the mascarpone.

2 In a clean, dry bowl, whisk the egg whites until stiff but not dry, then, using a large metal spoon, gently fold into the egg yolk mixture together with the torrone and all but 2 tablespoons of the chocolate, if using. Spoon a layer over the bottom of a serving bowl.

3 In a shallow dish, stir together the coffee and liqueur. Dip one sponge finger into the dish for 10–15 seconds, turning it over so it is well soaked but does not become soggy. Place on the mascarpone mixture. Repeat with 5 more fingers, arranging them side by side. Cover with one third of the remaining mascarpone mixture. Make two more layers of fingers and mixture in the same way, then cover the top with the remaining mascarpone mixture.

4 Sprinkle the remaining chocolate, or cocoa powder if chocolate is not being used, evenly over the mascarpone. Chill in the refrigerator for at least 3 hours. Return to room temperature about 30 minutes before serving.

Illustrated opposite page 145

MUSCAT WINE JELLY AND CREAM

SERVES 4

If you think of jelly as being made from artificially-flavoured and coloured cubes from a packet and fit only for children's parties, you are in for a surprise. This one is very much for adults. The jelly is made with a wine that has a wonderful, rich, fresh, fruity, muscat flavour, with a sweetness that comes naturally from the grapes and not added by man. I often set it in sweet, juicy ripe Charentais or Ogen melons, but if they are not available, the jelly can be set in glasses and partnered by other sweet, juicy fruits.

- 310 ML/11 FL OZ WATER
- 2½ TSP POWDERED GELATINE
- 100 G/3½ OZ CASTER SUGAR
- 400 ML/14 FL OZ MUSCAT WINE, SUCH AS MUSCAT DE RIVESALTES, DE FRONTIGNAN OR BEAUMES-DE-VENISE
- JUICE OF ½–1 LEMON
- 2 SMALL, RIPE CHARENTAIS OR OGEN MELONS

TO SERVE:

- APPROXIMATELY 85–115 ML/3–4 FL OZ SINGLE CREAM, CHILLED

Using a sharp knife, cut a deep zig-zag line around the circumference of the melon

1 Put 55 ml/2 fl oz water into a small heatproof bowl, sprinkle the gelatine over the top and leave for about 5 minutes until spongy. Place the bowl over a saucepan of hot water and leave until the gelatine has dissolved.

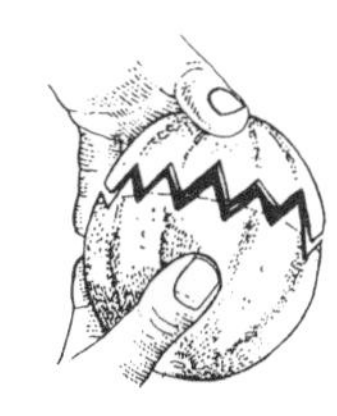

Separate the two halves

2 Meanwhile, put the sugar, wine and the remaining water into a saucepan and heat, stirring occasionally, until the sugar has dissolved.

3 Remove the bowl containing the gelatine from the pan and leave to cool slightly. Stir in a little of the wine mixture, then stir back into the remaining wine mixture. Add lemon juice to taste, then leave in a cool place until thick and syrupy.

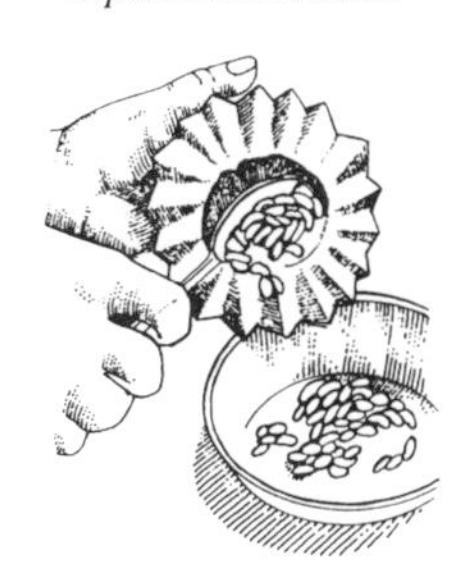

Using a spoon, scoop out the seeds

4 Using a small sharp knife, and working around the equator of each melon, make a series of long, zigzag cuts to cut the melons in half. Scoop out and discard the seeds and fibres from the centre of each melon.

5 Reserve about one quarter of the jelly and divide the remainder between the melon shells. Place with the reserved jelly in the refrigerator to set.

6 Just before serving, whip the reserved jelly until frothy. Spoon on top of the jelly in the melon, then serve with single cream poured over.

VOLUPTUOUS CHESTNUT, CHOCOLATE AND RUM CAKE

SERVES 8

Chestnut trees were known as bread trees and the nuts were a staple of many peasant communities in France, Italy and Spain because they can be used in several different forms – fresh, dried, whole, puréed and ground to a flour – and in many different dishes, both sweet and savoury. But this cake certainly did not emanate from a peasant kitchen! The complete recipe as I have given it fully exploits the way chestnuts and chocolate enhance each other and it is one of life's most wonderful eating experiences. The cake on its own, with no more than a dusting of icing sugar and cocoa powder, makes a special pudding, so the filling and icing are really an extravagance that 'gilds the lily'. But why not?

- 115 G/4 OZ BITTER CHOCOLATE, CHOPPED
- 55 G/2 OZ UNSALTED BUTTER, DICED
- 250 G/9 OZ UNSWEETENED CHESTNUT PURÉE
- FEW DROPS VANILLA ESSENCE
- 4 EGGS, SEPARATED
- 55 G/2 OZ CASTER SUGAR
- 1 EGG WHITE
- 4 TBSP DARK RUM
- **FILLING (OPTIONAL):**
  150 ML/5 FL OZ DOUBLE OR WHIPPING CREAM
- 1 TBSP VANILLA CASTER SUGAR
- APPROXIMATELY 40 G/1½ OZ COOKED CHESTNUTS, CHOPPED (SEE PAGE 138)
- **ICING (OPTIONAL):**
- 175 G/6 OZ PLAIN CHOCOLATE, CHOPPED
- 4 TBSP WATER
- 55 G/2 OZ UNSALTED BUTTER, DICED
- **DECORATION:**
- MARRONS GLACÉS
- CRYSTALLIZED ANGELICA (OPTIONAL)

1 Set the oven to 180°C/350°F/Gas 4. Line the base and sides of a 20 cm/8 inch diameter, 5 cm/2 inch deep cake tin with greaseproof paper, then butter the paper.

2 Place the chocolate and butter in a medium-sized heatproof bowl and place over a saucepan of hot water. Stir occasionally until the chocolate and butter have melted and the mixture is smooth. Remove from the heat and sieve in the chestnut purée. Add a few drops of vanilla essence and stir to mix.

3 In a separate bowl, whisk the egg yolks and sugar until thick and pale, then, using a large metal spoon, gently fold into the chocolate mixture.

4 In a clean, dry bowl, whisk the egg whites until stiff but not dry, then, with the metal spoon, gently fold into the chocolate mixture. Transfer to the cake tin and bake for 50 minutes until springy to the touch in the centre.

5 Remove the cake from the oven and pierce holes over the top. Spoon over the rum and leave to cool in the tin.

6 Remove the cake from the tin and carefully peel off the lining paper. When cold, slice the cake in half horizontally.

7 To make the filling, lightly whip the cream with the sugar, then gently fold in the chestnuts. Spread over one half of the cake, then cover with the other half.

8 To make the icing, melt the chocolate with the water in a heatproof bowl and place over a saucepan of hot water. When smooth, remove the bowl from the saucepan and gradually beat in the butter. Leave to cool until beginning to thicken, then quickly pour over the cake and spread down the sides using a palette knife. Decorate with marrons glacés and crystallized angelica, if liked, and leave to set.

Illustrated opposite page 160

SAUCES

CHAPTER SIX

The right sauce is a valuable asset to a pudding and should complete it and be part of it, not simply an adjunct to it. This means marrying or contrasting flavours, textures and consistencies so that together they are better than the sum of their individual parts. A sauce can also, of course, moisten a pudding, but it should not swamp it – unless the sauce is superior to the pudding!

CUSTARD

Custard is the most traditional and most frequently served pudding sauce. To make proper egg-based custard does not require skill, just a little patience, but this will be well rewarded by the taste and texture of the finished sauce and its effect on the pudding, and the people eating it.

☞ Use a heavy-based saucepan. I like to use one that has a non-stick coating. If using an ordinary saucepan, rinsing the pan with cold water before starting helps to prevent the milk or cream 'catching'.

☞ The base of the pan must be completely flat for even cooking.

☞ A vanilla pod can be re-used. Simply rinse and dry it after removing it from the milk or cream, then return the pod to its container.

☞ When using a vanilla pod to flavour a custard, the strength of flavour is controlled by the length of time the pod is left in the milk or cream.

☞ To ensure the heat is gentle beneath the custard as it cooks, a heat diffusing mat is useful. Some peole prefer to use a double saucepan or a heatproof bowl placed over a saucepan of hot, not boiling, water. If you use this method, check that the underside of the bowl is clear of the water.

☞ When stirring the custard, make sure you move the spoon or spatula across the entire base of the pan and reach into the angle between the base and the sides.

☞ If the custard looks as if it is beginning to cook too quickly or unevenly, remove the pan from the heat straightaway and stir hard.

☞ Custard can be made in advance and reheated if this is done in a heatproof basin placed over a saucepan of hot, not boiling, water. Stir the custard frequently while it is warming up. Custard thickens when it cools, so it may be necessary to add a little more milk or cream.

Wooden spoon for custard:

The corner of the spoon gets right in to the angle between the base and sides of the saucepan

Removing seeds from a vanilla pod:

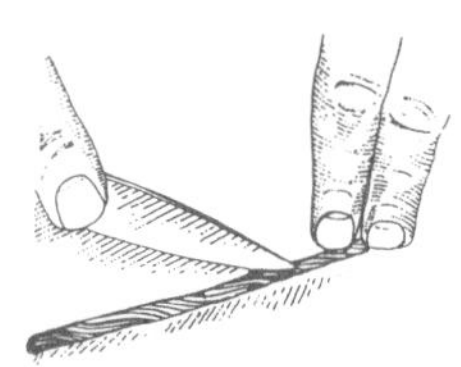

For a stronger vanilla flavour, slit the pod lengthways, using the point of a sharp knife

Scrape out the seeds and put the seeds in the milk to heat and infuse. Do not strain

Custard

SERVES 4

Many puddings benefit from being accompanied by a good custard, by which I mean custard made using eggs. Custard made from a packet mix certainly has the advantages of cost, convenience and simplicity, and many people like it, but I'm sure you'll find this version scores on flavour and texture, especially for special occasions. The richness of the custard can be altered by using single, whipping or double cream in place of some or all of the milk, and by using some whole eggs instead of all egg yolks (1 whole egg to replace 2 yolks), or even by increasing the number of egg yolks to 6 or even 8.

- 425 ML/15 FL OZ MILK
- 1 VANILLA POD OR A FEW DROPS VANILLA ESSENCE
- 5 EGG YOLKS
- APPROXIMATELY 40 G/1 ½ OZ CASTER SUGAR

1 In a heavy saucepan, gently heat the milk with the vanilla pod, if using, to simmering point. Remove from the heat, cover and leave for 15–20 minutes.

2 In a bowl, whisk together the egg yolks and sugar until thick and light.

3 Uncover the saucepan, remove the vanilla pod, if used, and the skin from the top of the milk. Bring the milk to the boil. Slowly stir into the egg yolks, then pour back into the saucepan and cook very gently, stirring with a wooden spoon, until thickened; do not allow the sauce to boil. Add vanilla essence, if using. For a really silky texture, strain through a conical sieve.

4 If serving or using the custard cold, pour it into a basin and leave to cool. To prevent a skin forming, either stir occasionally, or lay a sheet of cling film or dampened greaseproof paper on the surface of the custard, making sure there are no air bubbles.

5 The custard can be kept, covered, in the refrigerator for up to 2 days.

VARIATIONS:

COFFEE CUSTARD

At step 1, infuse 2 tablespoons of espresso coffee or finely ground dark or continental roast coffee beans with the vanilla pod in the milk. Follow the rest of the recipe as normal; do not strain the custard.

ORANGE CUSTARD

Omit step 1. Add the vanilla pod at step 2 when bringing the milk to the boil and remove it as soon as the milk reaches boiling point. Follow the remaining recipe to the end of step 3, then stir in the finely grated rind of 2 small oranges, and 1½ tablespoons of Cointreau, if liked.

CINNAMON CUSTARD

Use 1 cinnamoon stick instead of the vanilla pod and follow the recipe to the end of step 3. Add about half a teaspoon ground cinnamon.

HAZELNUT CUSTARD

Add 125 g/4½ oz ground, lightly toasted hazelnuts when the egg yolk and milk mixture has been poured back into the saucepan prior to cooking until thickened. Do not strain.

PRALINE CUSTARD

As for Hazelnut Custard, substituting crushed praline powder (see page 42).

RUM, WHISKY OR BRANDY CUSTARD

Add 3 tablespoons of rum, whisky or brandy to the custard just before serving if serving hot; add when cold if serving cold.

CHOCOLATE CUSTARD

Add 55–85 g/2–3 oz chopped plain chocolate to the milk before reheating to the boil.

WHAT WENT WRONG?

☞ THE CUSTARD HAS CURDLED:
The custard will curdle if it is cooked too quickly at too high a temperature or it is not stirred sufficiently, especially towards the end of the cooking.

☞ THE CUSTARD IS TOO THIN:
This is caused by using an insufficient number of eggs or not cooking the custard for long enough.

*H*OT CHOCOLATE SAUCE

SERVES 4–6

This Hot Chocolate Sauce has a good, smooth, rich, chocolatey flavour.

- 200 G/7 OZ BITTER CHOCOLATE, CHOPPED
- 115 ML/4 FL OZ MILK
- 2 TBSP DOUBLE CREAM (OPTIONAL)
- 15 G/1 ½ OZ UNSALTED BUTTER

1 Put the chocolate into a small heatproof bowl, place over a saucepan of hot water and leave to melt, stirring occasionally.

2 Bring the milk and cream, if using, to the boil, then slowly stir into the chocolate. Remove from the heat and stir in the butter.

VARIATION:
For a Hot Mocha Sauce, use strong white coffee instead of the milk and add sugar to taste.

CHOCOLATE SAUCE

SERVES 4

Instant coffee granules, vanilla essence, orange liqueur, brandy, whisky or rum can be added to taste.

- 175 G/6 OZ BITTER CHOCOLATE, CHOPPED
- 4 TBSP WATER
- 15 G/½ OZ UNSALTED BUTTER, DICED

1 Put the chocolate and the water into a small heatproof bowl placed over a saucepan of hot water and leave to melt, stirring occasionally.

2 Remove the bowl from the heat and stir in the butter. Serve warm or cold.

VARIATION:
For a Chocolate Mint Sauce, use chopped chocolate mint crisps instead of bitter chocolate.

FLUFFY ORANGE SAUCE

SERVES 4

A billowy, tangy sauce that can be served as soon as it is made, or made up to 8 hours in advance and served cold. The wine not only contributes to the flavour, but also makes the sauce a little lighter.

- 3 EGG YOLKS
- FINELY GRATED RIND AND JUICE OF 2 ORANGES
- JUICE OF 1 LEMON
- APPROXIMATELY 55 G/2 OZ CASTER SUGAR
- 55 ML/2 FL OZ DESSERT WINE
- COINTREAU, TO TASTE (OPTIONAL)

1 Put all the ingredients together in as medium-sized heatproof bowl. Place the bowl over a saucepan of hot water, making sure the bottom of the bowl is not touching the water, and whisk until thick, foamy and doubled in volume; this will take about 10–15 minutes.

2 Serve immediately or remove the bowl from the saucepan and continue to whisk the sauce until it is cold.

SABAYON SAUCE

SERVES 4

The quality and character of the wine will affect the taste, and therefore enjoyment, of this sauce. Light-weight wines with a fairly high acidity, such as Muscadet, are the lowest on my list; a sauce made from a medium-sweet wine that is a bit 'flabby' because it lacks acidity, such as Liebfraumilch, can be improved by the addition of lemon, lime or orange juice. The sweetness of the wine will govern the amount of sugar needed, and the sweetness of the pudding should also be borne in mind.

- 3 EGG YOLKS, SIZE 2
- APPROXIMATELY 40 G/1 ½ OZ VANILLA CASTER SUGAR
- 115 ML/4 FL OZ FRUITY-FLOWERY DRY WHITE WINE, SUCH AS CHENIN BLANC
- LEMON JUICE (OPTIONAL)

1 Put the egg yolks, sugar and wine in a medium-sized heatproof bowl, placed over a saucepan of hot water and whisk until the mixture is pale, doubled in volume and almost thick enough to support a trail; this will take about 10–15 minutes. Add more sugar and lemon juice, if necessary.

2 If serving the sauce warm, serve immediately. If serving it cold, place the bowl in a bowl of iced water and whisk until cold.

BRANDY BUTTER SAUCE

SERVES 4

This is different from traditional brandy butter, as it contains an egg yolk and cream to give a softer consistency. It has a chameleon character, as it is just as at home with special puddings as with simple ones, lifting them to a higher level. It can be prepared in advance and, because it can be kept in the refrigerator for up to 1 week, it is a useful 'store-cupboard standby' for serving with innumerable puddings, from pancakes and waffles, steamed and baked puddings, to fruit puddings and for stirring into rice and similar puddings. Spirits, liqueurs and flavouring can be varied to complement the pudding that the sauce is to accompany.

- 115 G/4 OZ UNSALTED BUTTER
- 115 G/4 OZ ICING SUGAR, PREFERABLY VANILLA FLAVOURED
- 3 TBSP BRANDY
- 1 EGG YOLK
- 4 TBSP DOUBLE CREAM
- GRATED RIND OF ½ ORANGE (OPTIONAL)

1 Beat the butter until pale and light, then gradually beat in the sugar alternately with the brandy, until light and fluffy.

2 Beat in the egg yolk, double cream and fruit rind, if using.

3 Store in a covered container in the refrigerator for up to 1 week.

VARIATIONS:

For a Rum Butter Sauce, use light muscovado sugar instead of icing sugar and substitute rum for the brandy.

For an Orange Butter Sauce, use Cointreau instead of brandy.

For a Spiced Whisky Butter Sauce, use light muscovado sugar instead of icing sugar, replace the brandy with 3 tablespoons of whisky and add the grated rind of 1 small orange, 1 teaspoon of lemon juice, ¼ teaspoon of mixed spice and a pinch of finely crushed cardamom seeds.

Apricot Sauce

SERVES 4

Dried apricots that do not need to be soaked tend to be sweeter than the traditional ones that need soaking, but they do not give such a good, fresh fruity flavour. The sauce can be served hot or cold and can be kept covered in the refrigerator for several days.

- 175 G/6 OZ DRIED APRICOTS
- 350 ML/12 FL OZ FRUITY DRY WHITE WINE
- LONG STRIP OF ORANGE RIND
- HONEY, TO TASTE (OPTIONAL)

1 Put the apricots into a bowl, pour over the wine and leave to soak overnight.

2 Tip the apricots and soaking liquor into a saucepan, add the orange rind and sufficient water to cover and simmer gently until very tender; this can take up to 40 minutes, depending on the apricots.

3 Discard the orange rind and purée the apricots and cooking liquor. Add honey to taste, if liked.

4 If serving warm, reheat the sauce and adjust the thickness with water or wine, so that it has the consistency of double cream.

INDEX

T

V

W

Z